Eduardo Santos and the Good Neighbor

Eduardo Santos
and the Good Neighbor
1938-1942

DAVID BUSHNELL

UNIVERSITY OF FLORIDA PRESS
GAINESVILLE / 1967

Latin American Monographs—Second Series
Number 4

A University of Florida Press Publication

SPONSORED BY THE
Center for Latin American Studies

Copyright © 1967 by the Board of
  Commissioners of State Institutions
    of Florida

Library of Congress
  Catalog Card No. 67-65496

PRINTED BY STORTER PRINTING COMPANY
GAINESVILLE, FLORIDA

Preface

THIS MONOGRAPH is intended only as one small contribution to the study of recent Colombian-United States relations. It deals with a single brief period—the four-year term of a Colombian administration that was, however, a particularly significant one for this topic. Furthermore, it is largely a discussion of political, military, and economic relations at the governmental level, ignoring such factors as the structural relationship between United States trade and investment and the Colombian economy, and examining basic Colombian attitudes toward the United States only insofar as they were overtly expressed in press comments and political debate. Such an approach to the study of international relations is admittedly old-fashioned and incomplete. On the other hand, a good supply of published and unpublished documentation was readily available on the specific problems that I have examined. It had been largely untouched by either United States or Colombian scholars and contained, I felt, much significant data; I therefore resolved to make use of it without further delay, in the hope that the resulting product would be of direct service to any other historian or social scientist who might seek to present a broader view either of the relationship between Colombia and the United States or of Colombian internal developments.

The United States sources used consist almost wholly of diplomatic correspondence, both that which has appeared in print in *Foreign Relations of the United States* and the far more extensive unpublished records preserved in the National Archives in Washington. The Colombian sources are principally newspapers and whatever official documents were published during or immediately following the period under study (e.g., the ministerial *Memorias*). Thus the United States documentation and the Colombian are not exactly comparable. In particular, the reasoning behind Colombian official decisions, and the personal views of Colombian decision makers, can in many cases only be inferred, whereas the thinking of United States representatives in Bogotá and of higher officials in Washington is expressly stated, by and large, in the diplomatic correspondence. This discrepancy is regrettable, but it is probably less serious than might appear to be the case, since in Colombia, unlike the United States, the relations between the two countries were the subject of frank and intense political discussion which was duly recorded in the press. Not only this, but the political climate per se in Colombia was a key factor in determining policy toward the United States, whereas the United States public and politicians were usually content to let the diplomats take care of Colombian relations.

Different portions of the research on which this study is based have been supported by the Social Science Research Council and by the Penrose Fund of the American Philosophical Society. I wish to express sincere appreciation for the assistance received from both of them.

DAVID BUSHNELL

Abbreviations Used in Footnote Citations

DS	Department of State records, National Archives.
E.	*El Espectador*, Bogotá.
FR	*Foreign Relations of the United States.*
L.	*El Liberal*, Bogotá.
Leyes	*Leyes expedidas por el Congreso Nacional. Sesiones . . .*
MemEcNac	Ministerio de la Economía Nacional, *Memoria.*
MemHda	Ministerio de Hacienda y Crédito Público, *Memoria.*
MemMinas	Ministerio de Minas y Petróleos, *Memoria.*
MemRels	Ministerio de Relaciones Exteriores, *Memoria.*
N.Y.T.	*The New York Times.*
R.	*La Razón*, Bogotá.
S.	*El Siglo*, Bogotá.
T.	*El Tiempo*, Bogotá.

Contents

Introduction

N THE PERIOD since World War II, relations between Colombia and the United States have been always close and almost always cordial. During the late forties and the early and middle fifties, friction arose over the status of Protestants, including United States Protestant missionaries, within Colombia. More recently, the declining coffee price has become a sore point. Yet on the broader world scene Colombia has been a resolute ally of the United States against the Communist bloc (or blocs). She was the one Latin American nation to send a contingent to fight with the United Nations in Korea and was the first Latin American nation to receive Peace Corps volunteers. The greatest portion of her foreign trade has consistently been conducted with the United States, and the atmosphere has on the whole been favorable for American private investment. Nor have generally good relations existed only at the level of government policy. Although popular anti-Americanism could always be found, it has been less strident than in many Latin American countries.

Things have not, of course, invariably been so. In the immediate aftermath of the loss of Panama, relations at both official and unofficial levels between Colombia and the United States were the very opposite of cordial, and Colombia's strict neutrality—with pro-

1

German overtones—at the time of World War I was a sign that hostility had only partly abated. The country's own experience, furthermore, inevitably inclined many Colombians to view other instances of United States interventionism around the shores of the Caribbean in the worst possible light. However, the Thomson-Urrutia Treaty of 1922, whereby the United States offered $25,000,000 to Colombia in tacit atonement for its part in the Panama affair, did much to clear the air even if it did not erase all lingering resentments. At the same time, a steadily mounting volume of trade and investment was strengthening the economic ties between Colombia and the United States that not even Panama had seriously weakened. The decade of the twenties, in particular, brought a flood of United States private investment in Colombian government bonds and economic enterprises, all over and above the official indemnity payment. Petroleum investment, which began on a large scale just after World War I, was subject to intermittent legal harassment, and the banana interests of the United Fruit Company, which dated back to the turn of the century, were afflicted with violent labor unrest at the end of the decade. Nonetheless, the process of capital penetration had come to stay, and on balance it was considered beneficial both by the Colombian government and by the upper-class elite which in effect dominated political and economic life.[1]

One Colombian who took a strong stand in favor of rapprochement with the United States was the Conservative Marco Fidel Suárez, who as far back as 1914 had proclaimed his doctrine of the "Polar Star"—that Colombia should always look to the North, to the United States as both an example and a natural ally.[2] Not only was Suárez a sincere admirer of the United States but he felt that for economic and geopolitical reasons the destinies of the two countries were inextricably linked: therefore, he concluded, Colombians might as well make the best of the situation, and he himself

1. E. Taylor Parks, *Colombia and the United States, 1765-1934* (Durham, N.C., 1935), pp. 395-473; J. Fred Rippy, *The Capitalists and Colombia* (New York, 1931), pp. 103-98.

2. "El norte de nuestra política exterior debe estar allá, en esa poderosa nación, que más que ninguna otra ejerce decisiva atracción respecto de los pueblos de América. Si nuestra conducta hubiera de tener un lema que condensase esa aspiración y esa vigilancia, él podría ser *Respice polum*, es decir, no perdamos de vista nuestras relaciones con la gran Confederación del Norte." Quoted by Manuel Barrera Parra, in the introduction to Marco Fidel Suárez, *El derecho internacional en los "Sueños de Luciano Pulgar"* (Bogotá, 1955), p. 10.

was entirely happy to do so. As President of Colombia from 1918 to 1921, he worked fervently for the acceptance of the Thomson-Urrutia Treaty, and one motive behind his ultimate resignation from the presidency was his desire to facilitate its ratification.[3] In the ranks of the opposition Liberal Party there were men who also believed in following the "Polar Star." The most important of these was Enrique Olaya Herrera, who as Foreign Minister had helped obtain final ratification of the Thomson-Urrutia Treaty, later served as Colombian Minister to the United States, and in 1930 became Colombia's first Liberal president in nearly fifty years.

Olaya's presidency from 1930 to 1934 produced the closest political relationship that had ever existed between the two countries. To begin with, he personally liked the United States. In addition, he took office as the world economic depression was deepening, with a firm faith that a policy of scrupulously respecting United States interests would assure him whatever aid Colombia needed in overcoming the economic crisis.[4] He delayed his final decision as to the appointment of a Minister of Industries until he had word through the United States Legation that his choice was acceptable to the United Fruit Company.[5] He insisted on maintaining service on the Colombian national foreign debt after many other Latin American governments had already defaulted,[6] and longer than Colombia could really afford. He obtained from Congress new petroleum legislation specifically designed to meet the complaints of United States companies regarding their operating conditions in Colombia.[7] And in spite of all this and much besides, he received mostly praise, not aid, from the United States. Olaya obtained one substantial short-term loan at the very start of his administration,[8] and that was all. The day of governmental economic aid programs had not yet arrived, and though the State Department could urge private bankers to look with favor on Colombian requests, it could not legally compel them.

Not all Colombians had entirely shared Olaya's blind faith in the benefits of American friendship, and one who had not was his

3. Jesús María Henao and Gerardo Arrubla, *Historia de Colombia* (6th ed., Bogotá, 1936), p. 813.

4. Minister to Colombia Jefferson Caffery to Secretary of State, March 11, 1931, DS 821.00/781.

5. Caffery to Secretary of State, Aug. 4, 1930, DS 821.6156/81.

6. John T. Madden, Marcus Nadler, and Harry C. Sauvain, *America's Experience as a Creditor Nation* (New York, 1937), pp. 111-15.

7. Parks, p. 475.

8. Below, pp. 68-69.

successor Alfonso López, who served as president from 1934 to 1938. Himself an experienced banker, though a moderate leftist within the Liberal Party spectrum, López most likely would not have expected such generosity from the financial community to begin with, as did Olaya. To be sure, López was not in any true sense anti-American—he was merely a realist—and though he often talked the language of an economic nationalist,[9] he did little seriously to hamper United States trade and investment. On the contrary, he signed a reciprocal trade treaty with the United States which was strongly attacked by Colombian protectionists on the ground that it made appreciable reductions in Colombian tariffs in return for little more than a needless pledge that coffee could continue to enter the United States duty-free.[10] Even more notable in this respect was his try at oil legislation. The legislation sponsored by Olaya, though approved article by article by a United States petroleum expert before passage through the Colombian Congress,[11] turned out to have serious technical defects from the standpoint of the petroleum companies. These were greatly ameliorated by the petroleum law of 1936 even though the López administration, in drafting it, had carried out only cursory consultation with the companies; and an immediate result was a sharp increase in the activities of United States petroleum companies in Colombia.[12]

One major American enterprise that sorely missed Olaya was the United Fruit Company. López did not clear any appointments with it and in fact engaged in a running feud with it. For the rest, the main concrete difference between the Olaya and López administrations, from the standpoint of United States relations, was the loss of the peculiarly close personal relationship which had existed between the Presidential Palace and the United States Legation.[13] López just did not cultivate foreign diplomats, not even those from Washington, and in any event he was deeply engaged in an ambitious domestic program of social and economic reform—

9. E.g., in his nomination acceptance address (*T.*, Nov. 6, 1933).
10. *S.*, Feb. 7, 8, 9, 12, and 13, 1936; *Reciprocal Trade Agreement Between the United States of America and Colombia* (Executive Agreement Series No. 89, Washington, 1936).
11. Caffery to Secretary of State, Oct. 31 and Dec. 13, 1930, Jan. 2 and 28, Feb. 27, and March 4, 1931, *FR* (1931), II, 7, 10-11, 14-15.
12. Minister to Colombia William Dawson to Secretary of State, Feb. 21, 1936, Jan. 18 and Oct. 19, 1937, and Chargé Winthrop S. Greene to Secretary of State, Sept. 14, 1936, DS 821.6363/1244, 1246, 1253, 1261.
13. Dawson to Secretary of State, June 17, 1935, DS 711.21/924.

his "Colombian New Deal," or *La Revolución en Marcha* as he liked to call it—which took clear precedence over foreign relations. Certainly he did not look to the American State Department to underwrite his reform program in the way Olaya had looked to the State Department and Wall Street together to save Colombian credit in the depression.

The pendulum swung back in the opposite direction when López, in turn, handed over the presidential office to Eduardo Santos on August 7, 1938. Santos did not restore quite the same intimacy between Palace and Legation that existed under Olaya, but he cultivated closer relations than did López, and he entered upon programs of active cooperation that were to set lasting precedents. The rapprochement between Colombia and the United States which received its doctrinal justification from Marco Fidel Suárez and had its extreme expression under Enrique Olaya Herrera took final shape under Eduardo Santos.

Early Relations

DESPITE the long-term importance of the Santos administration in the field of foreign policy, the short-run significance of Eduardo Santos's inauguration as President
in August, 1938, was almost wholly domestic. Basically
a moderate on economic and social issues, Santos represented a
qualified shift to the right after the active reformism of Alfonso
López's Revolución en Marcha. Furthermore, Santos lacked the
partisan militancy of López. He sought to conciliate, and when he
pledged full political guarantees to the opposition, most Conservative leaders were initially disposed to give him the benefit of the
doubt. The López wing of Liberals had not wanted Santos in the
first place, but was nevertheless prepared to bide its time. Thus
Santos began his period of office in an atmosphere of relative good
feeling, which in turn was to prove of obvious advantage to him in
pursuing his chosen policy of close friendship and collaboration
with the United States.[1]

Before Santos left office in 1942, not only did the heat of do-

1. For a general discussion of the Colombian political background of the
period, see Vernon L. Fluharty, *The Dance of the Millions: Military Rule and
the Social Revolution in Colombia, 1930-1956* (Pittsburgh, 1957), pp. 43-65.
Though somewhat tendentious in interpretation and at times inaccurate in
detail, Fluharty's book is still the best treatment available of Colombian
history during approximately the second quarter of the twentieth century.

mestic political conflict rise again to dangerous levels, but the President's international policy became the subject of angry partisan debate. In due course, Santos was to be vilified as a mere lackey of the United States—as an *entreguista* in the worst tradition of Olaya Herrera. It is therefore worth noting at the outset that there had been a time when both Santos and his newspaper *El Tiempo* enjoyed the reputation of being not pro- but anti-United States. When the Liberal Party returned to power in 1930, United States representatives in Colombia still harbored definite reservations concerning him: Santos was "very anti-American," according to one intelligence report drawn up just a few weeks before Olaya's inauguration.[2] However, it was confidently expected by the same United States observers that his personal and party loyalty to Olaya would assure his support, or at least his acquiescence, for the latter's strongly pro-American policies. On the whole, this expectation proved to be well founded. *El Tiempo* continued critical of the United Fruit Company, proclaimed "South America for the South Americans," and favored suspension of service on the nation's foreign debt;[3] but fundamentally the newspaper did not betray any systematic anti-Americanism, only a reasonable regard for Colombian interests. In its main lines, certainly, the foreign policy of Olaya Herrera had the political backing of Santos.

Like most educated Colombians, furthermore, Santos responded positively to the Good Neighbor Policy as preached by Franklin D. Roosevelt, taking it as evidence of a sincere intention on the part of the United States government to mend its ways in hemispheric affairs. Nor was there ever the slightest doubt, as tension increased on the world scene between the European Axis dictatorships and the democratic powers, as to where Santos's sympathies lay. If he had not been a longstanding ardent champion of the United States, he was a notorious Colombian Francophile; and though he might feel attracted more to French than to Anglo-Saxon culture, he looked upon the United States as potentially the strongest defender of democratic values, which to him included both French and Colombian values, in the impending crisis.

I

The resolve of President Santos to work closely with the United States found prompt expression in the field of military cooperation,

2. Report of U.S. military attaché, Bogotá, April 1, 1930, DS 821.00/704.
3. *T.*, Sept. 12, 1930, Jan. 10 and 13, 1932, and *passim*.

and far from Santos merely doing the bidding of the United States, the initiative in the matter came from the Colombian side. Just two days after his inauguration, in talking to former United States Minister to Colombia Jefferson Caffery—who had been an official representative at the inaugural ceremony—Santos informally mentioned his interest in obtaining a United States naval mission for Colombia. He emphasized to Caffery that he hoped such a mission would not try to promote the sale of armaments and in this connection remarked bitterly on the success of earlier communications and aviation missions from Switzerland in unloading expensive equipment (much of it worthless, according to Santos) on Colombia.[4] Indeed Santos had not the slightest desire to embark on an arms race. The objective he had in mind was simply to assist the technical modernization and professionalization of Colombia's traditionally small armed services. At the same time, as he explained later, he intended the request for technical military assistance to be a demonstration of Colombian confidence in the United States.[5]

The State Department immediately expressed gratification over Santos's proposal and relayed to him an assurance that it was a fundamental policy of United States military missions not to engage in sales promotion.[6] There was a slight complication, to be sure, in that Colombia already had a British naval mission. The creation of the Colombian navy in its modern form really dates from the arrival of the British mission in 1935, and the British not only trained Colombian personnel but held actual command positions in the Colombian navy while Colombians were being prepared to take full responsibility. Colombia appears to have had no serious complaint over the British performance. Nevertheless, the new administration decided to replace the British with a United States mission, on the ground that United States technical advances and "greater facilities" made the change advisable. The details were quickly arranged, and on November 23, 1938, the necessary agreement was signed, to cover a four-year period. It provided that the United States naval mission, unlike its British predecessor, should function only in a technical advisory capacity, since British-trained Colombian officers were now available to hold

4. Caffery to Secretary of State, Aug. 9, 1938, *FR* (1938), V, 462.
5. Ambassador to Colombia Spruille Braden to Secretary of State, March 3, 1939, DS 711.21/931.
6. Secretary of State to Greene, Aug. 12, 1938, *FR* (1938), V, 464.

all positions of command. The British mission then terminated its services, and the United States mission began to function early in 1939.[7]

Though Santos originally mentioned only a naval mission, the negotiations were expanded to set up an aviation mission as well. Some years earlier, as a result of the Leticia crisis between Colombia and Peru, a number of United States pilots and aviation mechanics had contracted individually to assist in the temporary expansion of Colombia's military aviation and had served, in effect, as an unofficial United States aviation mission.[8] There had also been European air missions at different times, including the Swiss mission to which Santos referred in uncomplimentary terms; but there was no aviation mission in existence at the time Santos took office. In fact there really was not much of a Colombian air force. However, a United States-Colombian aviation agreement was worked out on much the same terms as the naval agreement (though for only a three-year period) and was signed on the same day, providing for a United States mission to help in the "development and functioning of the aviation of the Colombian Army."[9] On the other hand, Colombia did not at this time seek a United States technical mission for her land forces. Instead, Santos attempted early in 1939 to obtain a French army mission, primarily to offer instruction at the Escuela Superior de Guerra and similar institutions. The Colombians also hoped to send some of their own army officers to France for advanced training and study, but the full program of Franco-Colombian military cooperation never materialized, because of the developing crisis in Europe and then the actual outbreak of war.[10]

7. *MemGuerra* (1939), pp. 1, 35-37; *Naval Mission. Agreement Between the United States of America and Colombia* (Executive Agreement Series No. 140, Washington, 1939). The British mission was headed by a retired Royal Navy captain, and its members went to Colombia in a technically private rather than a British official capacity. See Basil O. Bell Salter, "Presente y futuro de la marina colombiana," *Revista del Ejército*, Oct., 1936, pp. 42-47.

8. *Newsweek*, April 21, 1934, p. 14; *MemGuerra* (1935), p. 12; *MemGuerra* (1936), p. 108.

9. *Military Mission. Agreement Between the United States of America and Colombia* (Executive Agreement Series No. 141, Washington, 1939).

10. *MemGuerra* (1939), p. xvi; *MemGuerra* (1940), pp. xvi-xix; *MemGuerra* (1941), pp. xxviii, 52. There had, of course, been earlier army missions too, including the Chilean mission originally contracted by Rafael Reyes which played a key role in the conversion of the Colombian army into a modern professionalized force.

By a curious coincidence, on the very day after the signing of the two mission agreements, Colombia revealed that her minister-designate was being withdrawn from Berlin as the result of an incident in which he and his party were temporarily detained by the German authorities for taking photographs of Nazi atrocities against the Jewish community.[11] There was no direct connection between the two developments, but their timing neatly symbolized the convergence of two aspects of Colombian foreign policy: an underlying disapproval and distrust of the Axis powers and a basic alignment in world affairs alongside the United States, with the one serving continually to reinforce the other. In the long run, moreover, the November, 1938, agreements represented an obviously important landmark in the history of United States-Colombian relations. They laid the basis for close collaboration in one of the most sensitive areas of national policy, and they not only set a precedent in this respect but inaugurated an era, for they have been extended repeatedly—and enlarged—from 1938 to the present.

News of the agreements was not officially announced until November 26. They were then greeted with uniform approval by the Liberal press, with a commentator in the President's own *El Tiempo* noting how appropriate it was to obtain military advice from a country such as the United States where the armed forces, as in Colombia, were traditionally subordinate to civil authority.[12] *El Siglo*, the principal organ of the Conservative opposition, took no formal position editorially on the agreements, although in between the signing and the announcement its editorials had been alluding to an economically inspired campaign by the United States to sell arms, while scoffing at the Axis peril to Latin America and adding for good measure that there was no difference between the "lynching" of Jews in Germany and of Negroes in the United States.[13]

Only on November 28 did the Conservative organ carry a full-length commentary on the subject, in the form of a special contribution initialed by the ultra-rightist Guillermo Camacho Montoya. It was, to say the least, an interesting performance, which started out with a frank acceptance of the need to obtain foreign technical help for the Colombian armed forces. But Camacho Montoya went on to assert that the missions had been contracted in the wrong

11. *T.*, Nov. 25, 1938.
12. *T.*, Nov. 27, 1938, and Nov. 29, 1938, in which the opinions of other Bogotá newspapers are reprinted.
13. *S.*, Nov. 24 and 25, 1938.

place. With regard to the naval mission, he stated only that the United States was not the world's leading naval power; he apparently preferred not even to mention the country that was. With regard to aviation he was less reticent, flatly acclaiming Italy as the most advanced country and thus the one best able to assist Colombia. "The Germans," he declared, "are also excellent aviators and have had the opportunity to train themselves in the open field of Spain." The Spaniards were excellent, too. Moreover, in case anyone should consider the technical inferiority of the United States an insufficient argument against the recent agreements, Camacho Montoya had an even more potent argument on cultural grounds: "The Saxo-American contribution to the cosmos of universal ideas is of an insufferable mediocrity. In their culture they offer only Poe and Whitman, two poets whose appearance on that scene was a miracle of nature. The United States will be exporters of civilization but not of culture. They have taught the world to shave, to take a daily bath, to use burnished toilets, to tar the roads so that the autos which their factories produce can roll upon them. . . ." After a discourse on the religious difference between Protestant America and Catholic America, he then offered his conclusion that it "would have been better for the government to contract these missions, which answer a need, in those countries with which we have greater spiritual affinities."[14]

One other contributor to *El Siglo* mentioned an alarming rumor to the effect that the mission agreements were somehow linked to an actual military alliance—"an impossible alliance," he called it— between Colombia and the United States. However, he accepted the prompt denial which had been published on this score in *El Tiempo*.[15] There, for the present, the matter was allowed to rest, since Camacho Montoya's outburst failed to set off any more widespread or full-scale campaign against the mission agreements. Nor did his personal preference for Fascist Italy as against the land of the Good Neighbor represent an exact consensus of Colombian Conservative opinion. It represented the attitude of an extremist wing which in bitter frustration over the existing Liberal hegemony in Colombia was increasingly attracted to anti-democratic doctrines generally and to the cause of the Axis powers. But there was still

14. S., Nov. 28, 1938.
15. Francisco Plata Bermúdez, "Una alianza imposible," S., Nov. 29, 1938. This particular rumor seems to have been first published by the Conservative *La Patria* of Manizales (cited in *T.*, Nov. 28, 1938).

a strong pro-American current in Conservative ranks, ultimately based on both the "Polar Star" tradition of Marco Fidel Suárez and the personal interests that linked many leading Conservatives with United States business firms in Colombia. This current found perhaps its purest expression in the small Catholic-oriented weekly *La Defensa Social,* which, if it had fulsome praise even for the United Fruit Company, could do no less than approve the United States military missions.[16] Somewhere in between was the most important Conservative of the period, Dr. Laureano Gómez, publisher of *El Siglo* and the acknowledged—though not unquestioned —leader of his party. Gómez, all things considered, was no admirer of the United States, but in recent years he had saved his bitterest denunciations for Nazis, Fascists, and Bolsheviks. He did not personally endorse every word that appeared in his newspaper; and though he would certainly have been happier without the two United States missions, it would scarcely have occurred to him to propose bringing an Italian mission to Colombia instead.[17]

The first heads of the naval and aviation missions reached Bogotá early in January, 1939,[18] and for a time they and their staffs were largely occupied with getting things organized and becoming oriented to the Colombian military scene. The orientation process had to be a mutual affair, and the naval mission, on its part, felt that the previous British advisers had tried to prejudice the Colombians in advance against their appointed successors.[19] But, on the whole, United States representatives were highly satisfied with the early progress of the two missions; and in practice military cooperation was not limited strictly to naval and aviation matters. The Santos administration does not seem to have shared the lively interest shown by the López regime in obtaining German equipment on liberal Nazi credit terms, and United States suppliers obviously stood to benefit.[20] Likewise, the Colombian

16. *La Defensa Social* (Bogotá), July 4, 1939. On the United Fruit Co., see, e.g., the issue of April 21, 1939. The fact that *La Defensa Social* was also blatantly anti-Semitic did not seem to conflict with its pro-American leanings; in fact anti-Semitism was a quite widespread Colombian phenomenon of the period (cf. the tone of comments on immigration policy in the *Memorias* of the Ministry of Foreign Relations, *passim*).

17. On the attitude of Gómez, see below, pp. 24-29.

18. *R.,* Jan. 11, 1939.

19. Braden to Franklin D. Roosevelt, March 27, 1939, DS 711.21/933.

20. Greene to Secretary of State, May 23, 1938, and Jan. 26, 1939, DS 821.24/104, 108.

government responded eagerly to an invitation to send a military commission—naturally including officers of the land forces—to visit Canal Zone defenses.[21] The visit took place in April, 1939, for one week, and was followed up by the return visit of a party headed by Major General David L. Stone, Commander of the Panama Canal Department, to Colombia in June.[22] The presence of Stone and his party inspired caustic comments from *El Siglo's* regular columnist on international affairs, "Américo Latino" (Luis Alfredo Otero), who cited Charles A. Lindbergh as authority in order to cast further aspersions on United States aviation proficiency after the fashion of Camacho Montoya and suggested that the only step still remaining would be for the United States to draw Colombia into an actual "military alliance . . . against the totalitarian countries, which would be a waste of time, since the dictators are more practical and alert [*avisados*], so that they exercise an economic and cultural penetration in America, more efficient than speeches about good neighborliness, democracy. . . ."[23] However, no such criticism could halt what was to become a continual round of inspection and consultation visits between Colombian and United States military men of all services.

In due course, various moves for reorganization of the Colombian armed forces were carried out on the recommendation of United States advisers; military aircraft previously condemned as unsafe were reconditioned, at substantial savings to Colombia; and while trips to and from the Canal Zone continued, an increasing number of Colombian military personnel were sent to the United States for specialized training. Naval officers, pilots, and aviation mechanics led the way, but infantry and artillery officers—and representatives of still other branches—were to follow. The training programs conducted by United States advisers in Colombia were also enlarged as time went on, even to the extent of sending noncommissioned officers to serve, at Colombian request, as military baking instructors.[24]

21. Braden to Secretary of State, March 3, 1939, DS 711.21/931.

22. *N.Y.T.*, April 13, 1939, 8:4, and June 8, 1939, 12:4.

23. *S.*, June 14, 1939. Although Fluharty, *Dance of the Millions*, p. 63, identifies "Américo Latino" as Guillermo Camacho Montoya, he appears to be in error. Cf. Rubén Pérez Ortiz, *Seudónimos colombianos* (Bogotá, 1961), p. 11.

24. Braden to Secretary of State, March 7, 1940, DS 821.20/131; *N.Y.T.*, Feb. 20, 1940, 8:5; *MemGuerra* (1939), pp. 38-39; *MemGuerra* (1940), p. xix; *MemGuerra* (1941), pp. xxx, 57.

II

A further innovation that dated from Santos's first year of office was the mutual raising of the diplomatic missions of Colombia and the United States from legation to embassy status. The change was recommended by Santos in his post-inaugural remarks to Caffery, and this proposal, too, had a favorable reception in Washington.[25] It became effective at the Washington end in October, 1938, when Miguel López Pumarejo, who had been previously serving as Minister, presented his credentials as first Colombian Ambassador to the United States.[26] The change in status of the United States mission to Colombia became fully effective early the following year.

The first United States Ambassador to Colombia was Spruille Braden, the same who later won lasting renown for his crusade against the Perón regime in Argentina. Braden brought to his new position a wide experience in Latin American affairs resulting from his personal business and financial activities, notably in Chilean copper mining, as well as from previous official assignments, although he had not yet headed the permanent United States mission to any Latin American country. He also brought a facile command of Spanish, a Chilean wife, and a genuine sympathy for Colombia, which he praised in a personal letter to President Roosevelt as the most democratic nation in South America.[27] His background in the field of business made him an eager promoter of United States trade and investment, but he knew the weaknesses as well as strengths of his fellow businessmen and was to prove a harsh critic of those who in his opinion were behaving improperly toward their host country.[28] The arrival of the first United States Ambassador was thus a positive factor in its own right—and in more ways than one—for United States-Colombian relations.

III

The favorable condition of relations between the two countries was underscored by the formal message of President Santos to Congress at its opening for a new session on July 20, 1939. Santos dwelt at length on the subject of inter-American cooperation and

25. Caffery to Secretary of State, Aug. 9, 1938, and Secretary of State to Greene, Aug. 12, 1938, FR (1938), V, 463-64.

26. T., Oct. 29, 1938.

27. Current Biography; Who's News and Why 1945 (New York, 1946), pp. 71-75; Braden to Roosevelt, March 27, 1939, DS 711.21/933.

28. Cf. below, pp. 97-98.

specifically emphasized Colombia's desire for United States technical aid in military and other matters.[29] He lauded the final abandonment of "imperialist ambitions" on the part of the United States and "the frank acceptance of a policy of sincere mutual respect, of explicit recognition of the sovereignty of others, of collaboration which excludes tutelage, which proscribes imposition and which does not protect undue exploitation. . . ."[30] He was careful to point out that Colombian friendship for the United States did not rest on any secret pact or understanding, but he also declared, in one of his most important foreign-policy pronouncements, that in the event of another world conflict Colombia could not remain indifferent to the security of the Panama Canal: "The Canal is one of the supreme routes of communication of the Continent; with its interruption our economy and all our standard of living would suffer a tremendous blow. We cannot say, because of a sense of proportion and because of the desire to maintain as far as possible a certain neutrality compatible with our interests . . . that we would come to its defense in case it was in danger of being attacked. What we do say, because it corresponds to our essential interests, our obligations as a sure and loyal neighbor, and the policy of American solidarity, is that no one will be allowed to menace the security of the Canal from Colombian territory, directly or indirectly, in any form; that our soil will not be a fit place to carry on or to suggest maneuvers that are even suspicious in that sense. If the case should arise, the Government of Colombia will know how to prevent it, without the necessity of being asked by anyone, with all the firmness and efficacy that are required."[31]

Santos's comments on solidarity with the United States and on the Panama Canal in particular were favorably received, by and large, in both countries. When Secretary of State Cordell Hull replied to press questioning that he did not recall any official consultations with Colombia on the subject of canal defense,[32] he merely confirmed, indirectly, the Colombian president's flat denial of the existence of a secret alliance—a denial that proved particularly gratifying to Conservative opinion. Moreover, the general approval which greeted Santos's statement in Colombia was made evident the following month when the Chamber of Representatives

29. *Declaraciones presidenciales. Julio de 1939 a abril de 1941* (Bogotá, 1941), pp. 10-21.
30. *Ibid.*, pp. 19-20.
31. *Ibid.*, p. 20.
32. *N.Y.T.*, July 22, 1939, 3:3.

with only one dissenting vote recorded its confidence in his inter-American policy.

The vote came on August 19 after some days of debate that featured strong denunciations of the United States by Representative Silvio Villegas, a right-wing Conservative who had recently broken with the leadership of Laureano Gómez in order to attempt the formation of an independent nationalist movement. Villegas was especially bitter in his attack on the naval and aviation missions, which he pictured as a form of imperialistic penetration carried out on the "pretext" of defending democratic institutions: "We handed over the petroleum and the bananas, and now we hand over our aviation."[33] Villegas strongly implied that he, like Camacho Montoya the previous November, would have preferred to obtain any needed technical services from the Axis powers. However, the fact to note is that Villegas fought a lone battle. For the Liberal majority, a group headed by the future left-wing martyr—and old enemy of United Fruit—Jorge Eliécer Gaitán presented a motion strongly backing the administration in its cordial response to the Good Neighbor Policy of Franklin D. Roosevelt. The Conservative minority offered a resolution of its own which differed little in substance although carefully stressing the fact that Colombia supported Santos's policy toward the United States "on the basis of juridical equality." In the end, a resolution was adopted that incorporated elements of both Liberal and Conservative drafts and satisfied everyone but Silvio Villegas: "The Chamber of Representatives declares its conformity with the international orientation followed by the government, of close understanding with the American nations and harmony and collaboration with the good neighbor policy proclaimed by the current president of the United States, founded in international juridical equality and unity of action for the defense of democracy and of the continent."[34]

Just four days later, Camacho Montoya again had free rein in the columns of El Siglo to laud Adolf Hitler as "the first political figure of his epoch" and providential restorer of Germany's greatness—all apropos the negotiation of the Hitler-Stalin pact.[35] But the overwhelming vote of the Chamber of Representatives for the defense of continental democracy was a better indicator of the state of political opinion at that moment. In the Congressional

33. S., Aug. 19, 1939. See also S., Aug. 12, 1939, and *passim*.
34. T. and S., Aug. 23, 1939.   35. S., Aug. 23, 1939.

debate, Conservatives had been more sparing than Liberals in praise of the United States, but they felt at the very least that hardheaded realism required Colombia to seek good relations with her wealthy and powerful neighbor,[36] and they were satisfied that Santos was doing so on terms compatible with Colombian interests and dignity. Moreover, the net effect of the Hitler-Stalin pact was certainly even more damaging to the Nazi image among Conservatives than among the Liberals.[37]

When war finally came, sentiment was predominantly pro-Allied among members of both Colombian parties (though more vigorously so in the Liberal camp). Minor anti-German incidents confirmed the uniform opinion of qualified observers to this effect; positive expressions of support for the German cause could be found in the *Karibischer Beobachter* published at Barranquilla but elsewhere were few and far between.[38] Colombian sentiment was even more overwhelming in favor of strict official neutrality, so that when Santos proclaimed such a policy in a decree of September 6, 1939,[39] he had with him the clear mandate of public opinion. Neutrality, however, was logically compatible with continued close collaboration with the United States, whose government formally proclaimed the same policy. Indeed, effective neutrality was thought to require such collaboration, precisely to ward off any possible threat to the peace of the hemisphere. Thus Colombia participated wholeheartedly when the United States promptly called a meeting of foreign ministers of the American republics at Panama. Her delegation readily approved the special neutrality measures adopted there, of which the most important was the proclamation of a neutrality zone—supposedly to be kept free from all "commission of hostile acts" or "belligerent activities" by the warring powers—that extended an average of 300 miles from the shores of the Americas.[40]

36. See, e.g., the remarks of Rep. Uribe Cualla, S., Aug. 12, 1939.
37. See, e.g., the signed editorial by Aquilino Villegas, S., Aug. 24, 1939, and the swastika combined with hammer and sickle illustrating p. 1, S., Aug. 25, 1939.
38. Braden to Secretary of State, Oct. 26, 1939, DS 821.00/1276; Braden to Secretary of State, Feb. 27, 1940, attaching copy of *Karibischer Beobachter*, DS 821.00N/50.
39. *MemRels* (1940), p. 3.
40. World Peace Foundation, *Documents on American Foreign Relations: July 1939-June 1940* (Boston, 1940), pp. 115-19; J. Lloyd Mecham, *The United States and Inter-American Security, 1889-1960* (Austin, Tex., 1961), pp. 182-85.

IV

For Colombia, joint action with the United States to cope with the war emergency took many different forms. Of greatest immediate concern to the Colombian government and people was the search for ways to lessen the economic impact of the European struggle,[41] but there was also intensified consultation on political and military aspects of national defense, including defense against Axis subversion and espionage.

President Santos himself had expressed a resolve to keep close watch over German, Italian, and Japanese activities from the very time of his inauguration,[42] but he did not originally assign much urgency to the matter. In March, 1939, he assured Ambassador Braden that the Germans and Italians in Colombia were behaving quite properly, although he had some reservations about the Japanese. He also attested to the genuineness of the anti-Nazi leanings of Laureano Gómez, even while recognizing that the European Axis powers might succeed in influencing Colombian Conservatives through their common attachment to the cause of the Franco regime.[43] Other Colombians were more inclined to view with alarm, including the Pasto city council, which in September, 1938, urged citizens and local authorities throughout Colombia to make Nazi-sympathizing German residents feel unwelcome—and voted to send a copy of its resolution to Franklin D. Roosevelt, among others.[44] The small Communist minority likewise made much of the danger from Axis agents and sympathizers,[45] particularly in the period before the Hitler-Stalin pact. But Santos's attitude was more typical. Then, after the outbreak of war, this same threat began to attract greater attention; and the first major impact of the changed atmosphere was felt by the Sociedad Colombo-Alemana de Transportes Aéreos (scadta).

Established in 1919 at Barranquilla by a Colombian-German-Austrian group, scadta was the oldest and one of the most successful commercial aviation companies in South America. It had filled a critical need in a country such as Colombia where topography was highly unfavorable to land transportation; and most Colom-

41. Below, pp. 72-73, 83-86.
42. Caffery to Secretary of State, Aug. 9, 1938, *FR* (1938), V, 463.
43. Braden to Secretary of State, March 3, 1939, DS 711.21/931.
44. *Tierra* (Bogotá), Oct. 14, 1938.
45. *Tierra, passim.*

bians from President Santos down looked upon SCADTA with a mixture of gratitude, affection, and even pride. The firm's official title had been something of a misnomer since 1931, when Pan American Airways acquired a majority financial interest. However, Pan American was mainly interested in assuring operating rights in Colombia for itself and in blocking the expansion of SCADTA outside the country in competition with its own routes; with these objectives satisfied through its ultimate control over SCADTA, Pan American was content to leave the previous management in charge of the air line's operations.[46] Thus a majority of key administrative personnel, pilots, and technicians continued to be German or Austrian, and though some were by now long-established residents of Colombia, others came out from Germany to serve for shorter periods. In such cases, they stayed long enough to familiarize themselves adequately with Colombia and then returned home, often to active service .with the Luftwaffe.[47] At the same time, through the aerial photographic service of which it had a virtual monopoly in Colombia, SCADTA was building up an unexcelled collection of aerial surveys. As journalistic alarmists were later to point out with monotonous regularity, these surveys covered some of the principal approaches to the Panama Canal. Indeed SCADTA aircraft had in the past flown over the Canal itself. Finally, SCADTA's private radio network augmented still further its potential to serve the interests of the Third Reich.[48]

It should be emphasized that it was SCADTA's *potential* for damage to Colombian and United States security, rather than any long string of clearly proven illicit activities, that gave rise to concern. However, for some time this concern existed almost solely on the part of the United States, not Colombia. Even in the United States, Pan American itself was long disinclined to interfere actively with the management of its Colombian subsidiary, which, from a purely operational standpoint, was creating no problems for the head office. Meanwhile Pan American preferred not to publicize the

46. Herbert Boy, *Una historia con alas* (2nd ed., Bogotá, 1963), pp. 62-63; William A. M. Burden, *The Struggle for the Airways in Latin America* (New York, 1943), pp. 11, 14, 27; petition of Pedro P. v. Bauer Chlumecky, Santiago, Chile, May 5, 1944, in Archivo de R. Botero Saldarriaga, Papeles relativos a sus labores en la Comisión Asesora del Ministerio de Relaciones Exteriores (Vol. I), at the Academia Colombiana de Historia in Bogotá.

47. Braden to Secretary of State, March 30, 1939, DS 821.976 SCA 2/408.

48. Burden, *Struggle for the Airways*, p. 68; *N.Y.T.*, Aug. 15, 1940, 6:3.

precise extent of its financial control, which had been reported to the United States and Colombian governments at the time it was acquired but still was not generally known in either country. There was considerable confusion as to the Pan American interest even among responsible Colombian officials. This confusion was encouraged, if anything, by the SCADTA management, and it was the United States Embassy under Spruille Braden—not Pan American Airways—that ultimately cleared the matter up.[49]

SCADTA was committed, in principle, to a policy of steadily upgrading Colombian personnel within the organization, but in practice the progress toward this objective was exceedingly slow. The first real move toward Colombianization of the air line came only in the closing weeks of the López administration, in the form of Law 89 of 1938, passed by the Colombian Congress, which required aviation companies operating within the country to employ a certain percentage of Colombians and also to be controlled at least 51 per cent by official or private Colombian interests.[50] The law allowed four years for the latter provision to go into effect, and a number of different proposals were put forward for the reorganization of Colombian civil aviation along the lines it laid down. The proposal that finally won official support—and was endorsed by President Santos in his message to the opening of Congress in July, 1939—called for the absorption of both SCADTA and the small Colombian-owned Servicio Aéreo Colombiano (SACO) into a new national aviation company with Colombian government participation.[51] This solution was perfectly satisfactory in principle to the German-Austrian group that had been running SCADTA. Indeed the passage of the law itself had been encouraged by the SCADTA management, some of whose members were already naturalized Colombian citizens while others were prepared to take the same step at any time. They apparently saw in the legislation a means of winning greater independence vis-à-vis Pan American and at the same time of protecting themselves against any undue interference with their affairs from Germany. Their confidence in their own position seemed fully justified when Santos himself helped expedite the naturalization of Dr. Peter Paul von Bauer,

49. Braden to Secretary of State, June 13, 1939, DS 821.79622/4, June 26, 1939, DS 821.796 SCA 2/417, Oct. 27, 1939, DS 821.796 Avianca/4, Dec. 20, 1939, and March 20, 1940, DS 821.00N/35, 55.
50. *Leyes* (Feb.-May, 1938), pp. 114-28 and especially 116, 125.
51. Braden to Secretary of State, June 13, 1939, DS 821.796 SCA 2/416, and July 26, 1939, DS 821.796/108; *T.*, July 21, 1939.

SCADTA's president and leading individual stockholder, which became effective in March, 1939.[52]

As far as Colombia was concerned, in any event, the law of 1938 was inspired by motives of economic nationalism, not fear that in its present form SCADTA posed a threat to security. Even after the law was passed, and even after Pan American finally gave instructions to the contrary, SCADTA continued recruiting pilots in Germany—and negotiating with the Nazi government to get them clearance to leave the country[53]—but Colombian opinion still reacted unfavorably to discussions in the United States about the SCADTA peril.[54] Reports of official United States pressure on Colombia to nationalize (i.e., de-Germanize) the firm produced a similar reaction. Such reports were flatly denied by the Colombian government in April, 1939,[55] and in a narrow sense the denial was no doubt accurate. But pressure was definitely being brought to bear on Pan American to do something about the SCADTA situation, as when Generals H. H. Arnold and George C. Marshall both made a point of urging the air line to replace German with American personnel.[56] Pan American never refused to cooperate. It was merely a bit too casual about the matter to satisfy United States officials.

The outbreak of war finally brought things to a head. United States official pressure was redoubled on Pan American, which at long last sent one of its top executives to Colombia to expedite the process of de-Germanization and to take part concurrently in negotiations for the establishment of a new national aviation company. With regard to the first of these objectives, the air line was clearly

52. Braden to Secretary of State, March 30, 1939, DS 821.796 SCA 2/408; Consul Nelson R. Park, Barranquilla, to Secretary of State, July 26, 1939, DS 821.796 SCA 2/419; Braden to Secretary of State, March 20, 1940, DS 821.00N/55. At first glance, it is hard to see why SCADTA officials should have feared interference from Germany when they could always successfully resist it, if they so desired, by appealing to Pan American. However, they were not all aware of the extent of Pan American's control; nor, apparently, was the German government. Von Bauer naturally was aware, but preferred to maintain the impression that he himself owned a controlling interest. On this aspect of the question, especially, see Boy, *Una historia con alas*, pp. 238-41.

53. Braden to Secretary of State, Oct. 27, 1939, DS 821.796 Avianca/4; von Bauer petition, May 5, 1944.

54. See, e.g., *T.*, Feb. 24, 1939, and Braden to Secretary of State, March 3, 1939, DS 821.796 SCA 2/405.

55. Braden to Secretary of State, April 25, 1939, DS 821.796 SCA 2/412; *N.Y.T.*, April 23, 1939, 27:2.

56. Memo by Laurence Duggan, March 17, 1939, DS 810.79611 Pan American Airways/1691.

unhappy, not only over the amount of effort required but also over the financial cost, including the liberal discharge payments owed to purged German personnel under the terms of Colombian law and company regulations. The cost was particularly high since the United States was determined that Pan American should make a clean sweep of naturalized German or Austrian personnel as well as non-naturalized staff members—so that von Bauer's new citizenship, for example, was not enough to keep his job for him. From the standpoint of Ambassador Braden, Pan American was still overly complacent, not to mention lacking in frankness. He charged that just as the firm had long refrained from spelling out the extent of its control of SCADTA, it now greatly exaggerated the difficulty of getting American pilots to take the place of Germans. Nevertheless, during the last months of 1939 and the beginning of 1940, more and more Germans were in fact let go and were replaced by either Colombians or Americans. All the top German (or ex-German) administrators were eased out in February, 1940, at which time SCADTA also installed special direction-finding equipment to keep careful track of the movements of aircraft piloted by still-to-be-purged German fliers.[57]

Although there was still much good will, official as well as private, toward SCADTA in Colombia, the Colombian government cooperated fully with the precautionary campaign that was under way. As early as September, 1939, it did its part by stationing military guards at civil airports and requiring Colombian military copilots on commercial aircraft flights.[58] Santos himself expressed solicitude to Braden for the longer established SCADTA Germans;[59] but he does not appear to have intervened more forcefully on their behalf.

Headway was also being made toward the establishment of a new aviation company that would replace both SCADTA and SACO,

57. Secretary of State to Sumner Welles, Oct. 6, 1939, *FR* (1939), V, 73-74; Braden to Secretary of State, Feb. 6, 1940, *FR* (1940), V, 729-30, and March 20, 1940, DS 821.00N/55; *N.Y.T.*, Aug. 15, 1940, 6:3. Pan American did ultimately receive compensation, from U.S. Army funds, for its special expenditures in the de-Germanization of SCADTA. See Stetson Conn and Byron Fairchild, *The Framework of Hemisphere Defense* (Washington, 1960), pp. 241-42.

58. *N.Y.T.*, Sept. 22, 1939, 4:2.

59. Braden to Secretary of State, Feb. 14 and 22, 1940, *FR* (1940), V, 731-32. Naturally, there were other Colombians, especially on the far right of the political spectrum, who expressed solicitude also for Colombian national sovereignty, which they felt was being sacrificed in the SCADTA affair to the pressures of Yankee imperialism (e.g., *Veritas* [Chiquinquirá], Feb. 14, 1940).

in line with Santos's proposal to Congress in July, 1939. The Colombian government was determined to have the dominant voice in such a firm but was not in a position to put in at once a corresponding share of its capital. The formula that finally was adopted called for the government to hold an option to acquire 40 per cent of the stock, with another 20 per cent ultimately reserved to private citizens who were native Colombians. In the meantime, Pan American Airways would remain the principal stockholder, and technical direction, at least for the present, would be exercised by Pan American personnel; but the Colombian government was to have from the outset a considerably larger representation on the board of directors than its stockholdings alone would warrant. The solution was not satisfactory in all respects to Pan American, but its freedom to bargain was limited both by the existence of the nationalization law of 1938 and by pressure from the State Department. Accordingly, on June 8, 1940, SCADTA was formally absorbed into the new Aerovías Nacionales de Colombia (Avianca), which was organized along the lines indicated.[60] By that time, moreover, the original German staff had been eliminated from all sensitive positions. Some German clerical employees remained, but they too were gradually removed over the following months, with the United States discreetly encouraging the exodus through continuing discussions with both Pan American and Avianca officials.[61]

60. Braden to Secretary of State, Oct. 27, 1939, DS 821.796 Avianca/4, Feb. 14 and 22, 1940, *FR* (1940), V, 730-33; Secretary of State to Braden, Feb. 2 and 6, 1940, *FR* (1940), V, 723-26, 728-29; Oliver J. Lissitzyn, *International Air Transport and National Policy* (New York, 1942), p. 332; *T.*, June 9, 1940.

61. *FR* (1940), V, 734n. Not quite one year later, the process was rounded out by Avianca's purchase of the small Aerovías Ramales Colombianas, which had been founded by a former SCADTA chief pilot (*FR* [1940], V, 733n, 735n).

The Good Neighbor Policy and Colombian Politics

D ESPITE some Conservative sniping at the military mission agreements and more general Colombian skepticism concerning United States assessments of the SCADTA peril, United States-Colombian relations inspired rather little controversy in either country during the period from the inauguration of Santos until shortly after the Panama Conference. But once the Colombian Senate began full-dress debate on the results of the Conference, a definite change could be seen. Colombian foreign policy, and Colombian-United States relations in particular, became one of the main arenas of combat between the Santos administration and the Conservative opposition, and later developments only intensified the argument.

I

The principal architect of the change was the Conservative leader Laureano Gómez, who took the initiative in making policy toward the United States a partisan political issue. Up to a point this merely reflected a gradual deterioration in inter-party relations on the domestic scene, which encouraged Gómez to seize upon foreign policy, when a proper occasion presented itself, as one more weapon of attack against the Liberal regime. But there was more to it than that. As already suggested in the previous chapter, Gómez's underlying attitude toward the United States was more unfavorable than favorable; and it did not take much to bring him into open antagonism on a given issue.

To be sure, Gómez never had been—and never would be—primarily interested in foreign relations. At the moment his one abiding passion was to maintain the strength and morale of the Conservative Party in its temporary adversity and thus be prepared to seize on any Liberal weakness or misstep that might pave the way for the Conservatives' return to power. And though he might take a dim view of the United States, he also took a dim view of the European totalitarian dictatorships, both Nazi-Fascist and (especially) Communist. He had even written a book, *El cuadrilátero*,[1] in which he assailed Hitler, Stalin, and Mussolini and held up Gandhi (of all people) as an example to emulate. That work appeared in 1935, and by 1939 he could have changed his opinions to some extent; for one thing, he undoubtedly felt some gratitude toward Hitler and Mussolini for their participation in the Spanish Civil War on behalf of General Franco, whose regime had the wholehearted support of Gómez as of virtually all Colombian Conservatives. Nevertheless, Gómez was still more anti- than pro-Nazi-Fascist. He regarded the German and Italian dictatorships as unscrupulous, inherently aggressive—at least on their side of the Atlantic—and blasphemously addicted to what his newspaper *El Siglo* termed "statolatry" (*estatolatría*).[2]

With regard to the United States, Gómez was not primarily concerned with the threat of Yankee economic exploitation. He

1. Bogotá, 1935.
2. S., Feb. 24, 1939. In the declarations of Laureano Gómez it is possible to find support both for the view that he was a sincere friend of democracy and the United States and for the view that he was a hardened totalitarian and pro-Nazi. It is particularly easy to do so if one holds Gómez personally responsible for everything that ever appeared in *El Siglo*. In the following discussion of Gómez's thought, therefore, I have been guided by my own impression of the persistent themes. That impression, in turn, is based principally on Gómez's own statements made in Colombian Senate debates during the period under consideration, i.e., 1939-1940; since these were most fully reported in his own newspaper, the reference (unless otherwise specified) is S., *passim*. If it should appear that in this study disproportionate attention is given to analyzing the attitudes of Gómez—to the neglect of the viewpoint of the Santos administration and other shades of both Liberal and Conservative opinion—the explanation is that it was Gómez who took the offensive, and also that his position on foreign affairs has been repeatedly subject to distortion.

shared with many Liberals the view that Olaya Herrera had been guilty of *entreguismo* in economic and financial matters, and *El Siglo* was generally hostile to United States petroleum companies in Colombia (although an organ of the ultra-nationalist lunatic fringe still described it as a "Conservative daily at the service of the great Yankee oil interests").[3] On the other hand, Gómez conspicuously refrained from harassing the United Fruit Company.[4] He, *El Siglo,* and Conservatives in general were resolutely on the side of capitalism against socialism; and they insisted with apparent sincerity that they favored any form of foreign private investment that did not seek special privileges in Colombia. Neither did he have any long list of concrete abuses to point out in the recent Latin American policy of the Roosevelt administration, though his admiration for the second Roosevelt was restrained at best. Looking farther back, he had not yet forgiven the first Roosevelt's "taking" of Panama, and he had bitterly opposed the Thomson-Urrutia Treaty.[5] But he accepted the fact that Panama, officially at least, was now a closed issue.

Nor, finally, was Gómez much given to rehashing the sorry record of United States military intervention elsewhere around the shores of the Caribbean. Indeed the one instance of United States intervention that, after Panama, most aroused Gómez's ire was one that left-wing anti-Americanists never mentioned at all: namely, the alleged intervention of the United States in Mexico *in favor* of the Mexican revolutionary government. Since the days of Dwight Morrow, he felt, the United States had been openly giving comfort to an anti-Christian and socialistic regime that was cruelly suppressing the *real* Mexico—the Catholic and traditional Mexico. Moreover, Gómez considered this to be just one aspect of a longstanding tendency on the part of the United States to oppose and undermine the forces of Hispanic, Catholic tradition in Latin America.[6]

Thus, in the final analysis, Gómez's distrust and dislike of the United States derived from what he felt was an unbridgeable difference in cultural values between Latin America on the one

3. *Colombia Nacionalista* (Medellín), May 26, 1939.
4. See below, pp. 88, 89-90, 96-97, 98-99 for further discussion of the attitude of Gómez and others toward both the banana and petroleum industries.
5. Felipe Antonio Molina, *Laureano Gómez, historia de una rebeldía* (Bogotá, 1940), pp. 216-20.
6. Braden to Secretary of State, April 27, 1939, DS 821.00/1272.

hand and "Saxo-America," as he often called it, on the other. "Saxo-America" was not only Protestant but wholeheartedly materialistic; Latin America was Catholic and was more responsive to things of the spirit. This analysis, scarcely original with Gómez, was also expressed by other Colombians of different political leanings, such as the right-wing Liberal Juan Lozano y Lozano (director of *La Razón*),[7] whose unswervingly pro-democratic and anti-totalitarian convictions were never seriously called into question. Nevertheless, Gómez proclaimed the thesis of United States materialism versus Latin American spirituality on repeated occasions and with obvious conviction. He insisted, with somewhat less conviction no doubt, that it did not make him anti-American, that he still found much to admire in the United States. He merely felt that cooperation between Latin America and the United States could only be in areas of concrete mutual interest, on a basis of mutual respect, with nothing to be gained by pretending that there was a general affinity of values and aspirations which in fact did not exist. For, culturally, Colombia's true ties were with Europe, not with the United States—and especially with southern Europe. Gómez saw in Germany the land of Martin Luther as well as of Adolf Hitler, and he asserted that England still had accounts to settle arising from Henry VIII's break with Rome and Elizabeth I's vendetta against the Spain of Philip II. As for the French, the France that he admired, like the Mexico he admired, was the one currently eclipsed by a revolutionary tradition he deplored.

In his approach to world affairs, then, Laureano Gómez was influenced more by dislikes than by likes. This trait led him as often as not to balance any criticism of the Axis dictatorships with a matching criticism of the western European powers or of the United States, and the result was to reinforce the isolationist tendency naturally stemming from his primary absorption in Colombian domestic politics. At the same time, he was prepared to tolerate a considerable diversity of outlook on international affairs within Conservative ranks, and certainly there was in this respect no dull uniformity to be found in the pages of *El Siglo*. The latter used the German Transocean news service (alongside the United Press), and its own foreign news commentator. "Américo Latino" was both persistently critical of the United States and generally understanding of the Axis viewpoint. *El Siglo's* women's page

7. Juan Lozano y Lozano, "Explicación de Colombia," *R.*, Oct. 3, 1939.

could gushingly proclaim, "Adolf Hitler Also Has Good Taste," apropos the design and furnishings of his Berchtesgaden retreat.[8] The paper characteristically minimized the incident leading to the withdrawal of the Colombian minister-designate from Berlin by suggesting that it was due at least in part to the natural resentment kindled in Germany by Colombia's undiplomatic official hostility. Yet on that same occasion even "Américo Latino" had to agree that Colombia's protest against the arbitrary detention of a foreign diplomat was technically justified,[9] and on still other occasions—though certainly not day in and day out—the editorial columns of El Siglo took a vigorous anti-Nazi line. An example of the latter was the editorial which appeared early in 1939 under the odd title "The Limitless Field of Senselessness" ("El campo ilímite de la insensatez"), and which undoubtedly reflected the thinking at that point of Gómez himself. It flatly denied that the basic conflict on the world scene was between Nazi-Fascism and Communism; it was between Christianity, with Catholicism in the forefront, and the "pagan and materialist" outlook on life which was a common bond of both Nazism and Communism. "If Russia has been the principal field of battle and of defeat of the Christian idea by the Communist enemy, Germany is the same [with respect to] the other enemy, paganism." The editorial then went on to list reasons for the irreconcilable opposition of Nazism to Catholicism and to give horrible examples of anti-Christian propaganda by Nazi spokesmen.[10]

With a few minor changes, an editorial such as that could just as well have appeared in a moderate or right-wing Liberal newspaper. Even so, one important difference between El Siglo's style of anti-Nazism and Liberal anti-Nazism was that the Conservative organ and its publisher Laureano Gómez did not necessarily like the United States any more simply because they disliked Nazism. Thus Ambassador Braden, after reaching Bogotá, expressed concern over El Siglo's general attitude, and as soon as possible he sought the opportunity to meet Gómez personally and see what, if anything, could be done to improve the situation. He arranged an interview with the prior knowledge and approval of President Santos, and in the course of it made reference to the unfriendliness of the newspaper, and especially of "Américo Latino." To this

8. S., Feb. 23, 1939.
9. S., Nov. 26, 1938.
10. S., Feb. 24, 1939.

Gómez predictably replied that neither he nor *El Siglo* were anti-American. He assured the Ambassador that Conservatives admired the United States as "the one perfect democracy," but that they felt the Latin and Anglo-Saxon cultures should develop along parallel paths rather than sharing the same path. He also made clear to Braden his resentment of United States policy toward Mexico. But the meeting ended on a friendly note, and it set a precedent for further direct attempts of the United States Embassy to influence Gómez.[11]

Though Gómez's newspaper continued to show certain hostile overtones and undertones, the harshest comments it contained about the United States were not as bad as the worst it had to say (on rare special occasions) about Nazi Germany. In the last months before the outbreak of war, the common denominator of opinions expressed in *El Siglo* about the world crisis was simply that it was no direct concern of Colombia. *El Siglo* held that Latin America was not really threatened—nor, in fact, was the United States, whose government agitated against the Axis to bolster its political standing at home and to advance its material interests in Latin America, camouflaging economic rivalry with ideological arguments. *El Siglo* observed that this same rivalry could prove only beneficial to Latin Americans, the implication being that they should play off one antagonist against the other in order to extract better terms for themselves.[12] Conservative representatives did, of course, give solid backing to the August, 1939, vote of confidence in President Santos's inter-American policy,[13] and this degree of party unity could only have been achieved with the concurrence of Laureano Gómez; but it is worth noting that the Conservatives in general, and *El Siglo* in particular, tended to place a strict interpretation on that vote. They related it above all to the President's self-evident proposition that Colombia could not permit her territory to be used for hostile acts against the Panama Canal, and insofar as they embraced inter-American solidarity, they chose to equate it at the present juncture with a common intention to preserve neutrality vis-à-vis European struggles.[14]

11. Braden to Secretary of State, April 27, 1939, DS 821.00/1272.
12. See, e.g., Nemesio García Naranjo, "La agitación bélica en los EE.UU.," S., June 11, 1939, and editorial, S., Aug. 17, 1939. An interpretation of U.S. motives in economic terms was also offered by Lozano (R., Oct. 3, 1939).
13. Above, p. 16.
14. See, e.g., "Cosas del régimen," S., Aug. 30, 1939.

II

The fragile structure of bipartisanship in foreign policy was broken when Laureano Gómez proceeded to denounce the Declaration of Panama as incompatible with the very principle of strict neutrality that it was supposed to maintain. Using the Colombian Senate, of which he was a member, as his primary forum, he charged that the neutrality zone established at Panama was a wholly unwarranted expansion of the concept of territorial waters which seemingly made it inevitable for Colombia to fall into the maelstrom of the European war. The war itself, he explained in rather muddled fashion, was just one more episode in the long conflict between northern and southern Europe; it was also one more expression of a prevailing modern-day materialism which would not be cured simply with the removal of a Hitler or a Stalin; and it was sure to be a long war, engulfing more and more peoples of the world as time went on. Colombia's only safe course under such circumstances was to "remain in a neutrality without qualifications." Yet under the Panama Declaration the presence of belligerent warships "hundreds of miles out at sea" could drag Colombia into the struggle. Worse than that, Colombia, though committed by the Declaration either to prevent or to punish an infraction of the neutrality zone, did not have the military resources to do so. Thus what the Declaration really meant, he claimed, was that Colombia placed her own territory at the disposition of the United States for use in enforcing its terms: "The day in which a German ship or a Japanese ship, or a ship of any nationality, decides to do anything, at a certain distance from the Canal of Panama, which we lost, it offends us! And we have to come to the defense of that which we lost, which is no longer ours, and as we have no means of doing so, we shall hand over our ports, we must hand over our air so that the Americans may . . . do us the favor of defending what is theirs. . . ."[15]

Gómez was not content with assailing the terms of the Declaration. He also accused the Colombian administration of assuming commitments for which it lacked constitutional authority, behind the back of Congress. Having given to understand that it was going to Panama to adopt measures for the assurance of neutrality, it had, he said, purely on its own initiative bound Colombia to a far-reaching and basically unneutral agreement which amounted

15. S., Dec. 6, 1939.

to a "real treaty of alliance"—something that, under the Colombian constitution, required Congressional approval. All this, Gómez concluded, formed part of an effort to "destroy the Congress"; it meant the "abolition of democracy."[16]

The official rebuttal to Gómez's charges, delivered in the Senate chamber by Foreign Minister Luis López de Mesa, correctly pointed out that Gómez grossly exaggerated the scope of what had been done at Panama. Colombia was not committed to any specific military action in case a German or Japanese warship engaged in "belligerent activities" within a certain distance of her coasts, much less to turn over Colombian bases to the United States for use in the defense of the Canal; by the Panama Declaration, Colombia was at most committed to "consult" with other American republics on violations of the neutrality zone, and López de Mesa held that this pledge was not unreasonable in itself nor was it in the nature of a treaty obligation.[17] He did not, however, convince Laureano Gómez. On the contrary, the statements of the Conservative leader in the Panama debate foreshadowed some even harsher criticism of Santos's inter-American policy that he was to offer later.

Even while Congress debated the Panama Conference, it was also considering a request from the Executive for extraordinary faculties in economic and financial matters to cope with the effects of the European war. The faculties were voted as requested on December 15, 1939, to expire on July 20 of the following year.[18] They were supported by a number of moderate Conservatives such as Senator Francisco de Paula Pérez,[19] an *antioqueño* of the "Polar Star" tradition and a lawyer for the Tropical Oil Company.[20] They were bitterly opposed by Gómez,[21] who thus expressed his lack of confidence in the administration in a field which had important foreign-policy ramifications. One such ramification was brought out by Gómez himself when he asserted that the same ally which might require Colombian collaboration in implementing the Declaration of Panama—i.e., the United States—was pressing Colombia to "accept money on conditions which we do not know and which the government does not want us to know, because it demands that we

16. *Ibid.*
17. *MemRels* (1940), pp. x-xxix.
18. *Leyes* (July-Dec., 1939), pp. 125-27.
19. *S.*, Dec. 14, 1939.
20. *Colombia Nacionalista,* March 10, 1939.
21. *S.*, Dec. 14, 1939.

delegate to it all the powers to negotiate. . . ."[22] Though he did not make the point explicitly, his remarks could easily be interpreted to mean that the surrender of Colombian sovereignty, as at Panama, was being purchased by the offer of new United States credits.

III

During the first months of 1940 no new issues of real importance arose to trouble relations between Colombia and the United States. Financial negotiations already in progress between the two countries continued without interruption despite Gómez's recent insinuations on this score, and finally began to yield concrete results in the form of specific arrangements both for the resumption of service on old debts and for the granting of new credits.[23] Military cooperation also proceeded for the most part uneventfully, although a minor controversy arose over the granting by Colombia of permission for the United States naval tender *Sandpiper* to be based at Tumaco while supporting two hydroplanes that were engaged—at the invitation of Ecuador—in an aerial survey of the Ecuadoran coastline.[24] *El Siglo* tried to portray this small courtesy in sinister terms.[25] However, by the time the *Sandpiper* issue came to the fore, in May, 1940, anything happening at Tumaco was easily overshadowed by news of the German spring offensive in western Europe.

None other than "Américo Latino" saw fit to express his personal preference, as of May 25, 1940, for the cause of the embattled western allies, "which is the defense of Christian civilization."[26] Presumably Laureano Gómez felt the same way, if he really had to make a choice. But when the initial German successes aroused new fears in the United States for the security of the hemisphere, and these fears in turn caused Washington lawmakers to expedite a measure for the supplying of defense equipment by the United States to Latin American countries, Gómez's newspaper was instinctively suspicious. Denying that there was any real danger of European aggression against Latin America, *El Siglo* stated in one of its blunter editorials: "The danger is elsewhere. The danger is in

22. S., Dec. 6, 1939.
23. Below, pp. 73-74.
24. L., May 29, 1940.
25. Braden to Secretary of State, May 31, 1940, DS 821.00N/63.
26. S., May 25, 1940.

initiatives like that of the American Senate, behind whose project an interventionist design pregnant with menace for our sovereignty raises its head."[27]

Such an outburst could be called neutralist or anti-American, but not in itself pro-Nazi. And Colombian sentiment generally, even in the face of the continued German triumphs that culminated in the fall of France, remained pro-Allied. Nevertheless, Ambassador Braden believed by mid-June, 1940, that he could detect a certain change in Colombian opinions. On the one hand, there had been a "surprising" increase in pro-Nazi feeling; on the other, friends of the democracies were sorely disheartened and would, he feared, be increasingly reluctant to take a strong stand.[28]

Undoubtedly some Colombians did decide on the basis of German military successes that there must be merit after all in Nazi ideology, but in other cases the upsurge in pro-Nazism consisted only of heightened efforts by the hard core of German propagandists and sympathizers already active in the field. One example of the latter was a flurry of clandestine flysheets urging Colombia to climb aboard the Axis bandwagon and thereby get back long-lost Panama.[29] In still other cases, what occurred was not so much an increase in positive sympathy for the Axis cause as mere acceptance of the likelihood of a final Axis victory joined with a measure of gloating over the present discomfiture of anti-clerical France and arrogant Britain. The weekly *Veritas,* published under the auspices of the Dominican fathers at Chiquinquirá, for two issues in a row depicted Hitler as a necessary instrument used by divine providence for the punishment of the ungodly. It aptly compared him in this connection, and with no apparent thought of flattery, to Nebuchadnezzar.[30]

Colombia's foremost Francophile, President Santos himself, put a somewhat different interpretation on recent events, but he was nevertheless badly shaken; he spoke privately to Braden of the "end of the British empire and France beaten to her knees." Foreign Minister López de Mesa, on his part, informed the Ambassador that Colombia despite her democratic sympathies would have to adjust herself to the material consequences of an eventual

27. S., May 31, 1940. On the "Senate project" to which reference is made, cf. *N.Y.T.*, May 29, 1940, 14:4.
28. Braden to Secretary of State, June 11, 1940, *FR* (1940), V, 60-61.
29. *N.Y.T.*, June 16, 1940, 28:2.
30. *Veritas,* June 19 and 26, 1940.

German victory.[31] Growing official circumspection was clearly reflected in a decree—issued immediately on the heels of an anti-Italian riot in Bogotá—flatly prohibiting demonstrations for or against any of the belligerents.[32] Even so, the official mood was hardly one of panic. The Santos administration did not seriously expect that even a victorious Nazi regime would unleash its armed forces on Latin America; it would concentrate instead on economic penetration and propaganda.[33] Nor did Santos waver in his basic commitment to collaboration with the United States. Thus military cooperation continued and was actually intensified;[34] and Colombia's delegation to the Second Consultative Meeting of American Foreign Ministers, which convened at Havana in July, 1940, duly gave its approval to the resulting agreements, including both the Act of Havana Concerning the Provisional Administration of European Colonies or Possessions in the Americas and the Declaration of Reciprocal Assistance and Cooperation for the Defense of the Nations of the Americas. The first of these provided for occupation of the territories in question if there was danger that they might change hands as a result of the European struggle. The second made clear that aggression by a non-American power against any one of the American nations would be regarded as an aggression against all. It was the first agreement of its kind to be directed specifically against aggression from outside the hemisphere, although it did not impose any binding obligation for military response but only for consultation.[35]

IV

The Havana agreements, unlike the Declaration of Panama, were submitted to the Colombian Congress for approval, but that was not enough to satisfy Senator Laureano Gómez. It merely spared him the necessity of rising to the defense of Congressional prerogative and allowed him to concentrate his energy on substantive questions. The problem of the European possessions treated

31. Braden to Secretary of State, June 11, 1940, *FR* (1940), V, 61. The quotation from Santos is Braden's paraphrase.

32. *N.Y.T.*, June 11, 1940, 2:6, and June 12, 1940, 8:3.

33. Braden to Secretary of State, June 21, 1940, *FR* (1940), V, 67-70.

34. Below, pp. 50-56.

35. World Peace Foundation, *Documents on American Foreign Relations, July 1939-June 1940*, pp. 93-95, and *Documents on American Foreign Relations, July 1940-June 1941* (Boston, 1941), p. 76.

in the Act of Havana he considered none of Colombia's business: those possessions had been piratically stolen from Spain back in the colonial era, and if some other power (which Gómez did not bother to specify) should now forcibly take away the loot from the original thieves—"if they pass from one exploiter to another exploiter"—the basic situation would not have changed. The provision that such territories, if occupied by the American nations, should be held only until they could be returned to their present owners or else given their independence did not sway his opinion in the slightest. Preventive occupation could be justified only with a view to returning them to the *original* owner or to that owner's successor states. Gómez thus had warm praise for Argentina's official reservation to the Act of Havana specifying her claim to the Falkland Islands, and he suggested that Curaçao, Aruba, and Trinidad should all have been earmarked for return to Venezuela.

Gómez was equally antagonistic toward the Declaration of Reciprocal Assistance and, more generally, the whole concept of mutual defense against extra-continental aggression. He did not renege on the Conservatives' earlier assent to the principle that Colombian territory must not be used as a staging area for an attack on the Panama Canal, but he flatly denied that Colombia had either a legal or a moral commitment to go beyond this in helping to repel an attack on the Canal or on other American territory from outside the hemisphere. Whereas he had previously ascribed a more sweeping character to the Declaration of Panama than it actually possessed, he now placed a very strict interpretation on all existing treaties that had to do with the peace of the hemisphere, and he was thoroughly unimpressed with the argument of López de Mesa, who informed the Senate that even before the Havana meeting Colombia already had a "spiritual" obligation, on the basis of both formal agreements and much else besides, to defend the hemisphere in general and the Panama Canal in particular against external aggression. The Foreign Minister did not greatly help matters when he sought to elaborate his remark by suggesting that Colombia was required, in effect, to offer only "spiritual defense," meaning evidently some kind of moral support or collaboration that stopped short of military action. Indeed López de Mesa's contribution to the debate on the Havana agreements was pounced on by Gómez and other Conservatives as proof of the dangerous fuzziness of the administration's thinking and thus adequate reason for lack of confidence in its foreign policy.[36]

In any case, Gómez insisted that the Declaration of Reciprocal Assistance adopted at Havana was framed for the benefit of just one American republic, the United States. None of the other republics was in any danger of extra-continental attack, and if the United States was in such danger—as he admitted to be the case—it was because of that nation's willfully unneutral posture since the start of the European conflict. As evidence of the latter he cited, among other things, the special relationship existing between the United States and Canada, a full-scale belligerent. And he posed the question: "Must we feel automatically aggressed against and suffer the consequences of what the United States did without consulting us or advising us? Why that? What logic has that?"[37]

Gómez did have some logic on his side, especially if one accepted his underlying assumption that an absolute neutrality was both desirable and possible. In this connection, his solution to the defense of the Panama Canal was to internationalize and neutralize it. He was perhaps less logical, or at least a good bit less lucid, in the long tirade against the concept of inter-American solidarity which accompanied his analysis of the Havana agreements on the floor of the Senate. Here he rehearsed the familiar theme of Anglo-Saxon materialism versus Latin American spirituality and asserted that in the realm of culture the United States had as yet produced no one to equal Colombia's own Miguel Antonio Caro and Rufino José Cuervo. To demonstrate the basic antagonism between the United States and Latin America, he gave a confused and in places fanciful account of United States efforts to undermine the moral fiber of Mexico from the time she became independent to the present, culminating in the encouragement given by Yankee ambassadors to the campaign of religious persecution (not to mention sexual education in the public schools) of the modern Mexican Revolution.[38] He had, however, struck a number of responsive chords among rank-and-file Conservatives. A veritable torrent of congratulatory telegrams poured into the offices of *El Siglo*, including one that read, "Si Cristo señaló camino salvación almas, usted sus discursos senado señaló camino salvación patria. . . ."[39]

36. *T.*, Aug. 13 and 14, 1940; *S.*, Aug. 13, 14, 20, and 21, 1940; *Anales del Senado,* Aug. 26, 1940.
37. *S.*, Aug. 21, 1940.
38. *S.*, Aug. 20 and 21, 1940.
39. *S.*, Sept. 9, 1940.

All this, moreover, formed part of a protracted Senate debate on foreign policy in which some other Conservatives outdid Gómez in the tone of their remarks. One of the most extreme expressions of anti-Americanism came from Senator (and later President) Guillermo León Valencia, who offered his own views on United States materialism, giving vent in the process to the common preoccupation of Conservative polemicists with Yankee "sanitary services," and ended by declaring: "We do not come to maintain that it is time to surrender to triumphant Nazism, but I would still say . . . that we have more points of contact with a political organization that wants at a given moment to organize the world so that all may have the same opportunities than with another which has considered that the world should be divided into exploiters and exploited; from this point of view we have more hope with triumphant Germany, that she may carry out a revolution of justice, than in the United States, that they may continue seeing in the 'dollar' the symbol [*cifra*] and the highest compendium of their civilization and their law."[40]

Administration supporters, meanwhile, dutifully defended the conduct of Colombian foreign policy, including the official commitment to inter-American solidarity. But the administration's chosen strategy was apparently to let the Conservatives talk themselves out,[41] so that the opposition was allowed, in effect, to keep the initiative in the debate. At the same time, discussion of the Havana agreements became thoroughly entangled with the debate that raged concurrently on a request that Santos had presented to Congress to authorize the borrowing of 30 million pesos for defense.[42] The primary object was to permit the acquisition of military equipment on credit in the United States, and Conservatives were not slow to ask whether that much money was really needed for a policy of "spiritual defense." The proposal seemed a virtual admission that Colombia had in practice become committed to more than "spiritual" cooperation, or else it was nothing but a senseless extravagance. Either way, it was bitterly assailed by minority spokesmen both in Congress and in the press. To *El Siglo* it was part and parcel of a contemptible "policy of docility

40. *S.*, Aug. 20, 1940. For a slightly different version, see *Anales del Senado*, Aug. 26, 1940.

41. Braden to Secretary of State, Sept. 15, 1940, *FR* (1940), V, 80.

42. *Anales de la Cámara de Representantes*, July 31, 1940. The Colombian peso, throughout the period covered by this study, was worth approximately 57 U.S. cents.

and servitude" whose logical outcome was to bind Colombia un-restrictedly to the defense of the Panama Canal, which in turn meant the defense of the United States, the very "power that mutilated her territory."[43] Or in the words of Representative Silvio Villegas—who by now had again found common ground with Gó-mez and the bulk of the Conservative Party—there was "no danger, no prospect of a German invasion against America. I believe that is a fable which is being exploited with expansionist ends on the part of the United States, and with mercantile and economic ends."[44] As explained by still another Conservative Congressman, the "economic ends" naturally involved the desire of the United States to unload a quantity of "scrap iron" in the form of obsolete arms on Colombia.[45]

One further complication at this point was the fact that the Liberal Party itself was becoming bogged down in dissension be-tween the followers of Santos and those of former President López, who were already maneuvering to obtain López's re-election to the presidency in 1942. López and his chief supporters were not opposed to hemispheric solidarity and cooperation with the United States, although they were critical of the defense-loan measure because they felt that Colombia's own resources and any financial assistance from the United States should be devoted primarily to internal economic development. Mainly, the lopistas were moved to harass the administration for reasons of domestic policy and for purely tactical considerations; but still their attitude was one more obstacle to forceful executive leadership. In spite of this, the loan measure—which at least had the eager backing of the Colom-bian military—did become law before Congress adjourned. In its final form it even provided that the amount of indebtedness incurred could go as high as 50 million pesos.[46] One lopista Senator

43. S., Sept. 7, 1940, and passim.
44. S., Sept. 7, 1940.
45. S., Sept. 5, 1940, containing the remarks of Rep. Rafael Azula Barrera.
46. Revista Javeriana, XIV (Oct., 1940), "Suplemento," 178; Braden to Secretary of State, Oct. 24, 1940, DS 821.00/1301, and Oct. 28, 1940, DS 821.51/2553; Leyes (July-Dec., 1940), p. 108. The reference made to the atti-tude of the military should not be taken as necessarily explaining the passage of the measure, since the influence of the military in Colombia was definitely limited at this point; Santos's desire to keep the generals and colonels both occupied and happy may, however, have induced him to work more vigorously for the defense measure than for the Havana agreements. (For reasons that will be noted in the next chapter, the measure was never actually used.)

had tried to insert an amendment earmarking part of the proceeds for agricultural development, but his proposal did not prosper, and in the end the López bloc went along with the administration.[47] The Havana agreements were less fortunate. They were still pending when Congress closed its sessions for the year and were formally ratified only in 1941.[48]

One thing both bands of Liberals managed to agree upon was that the Conservatives had turned obstructionist in the field of international relations under the influence of news from Europe. The Conservative vote of confidence in Santos's inter-American policy in August, 1939, was contrasted with the Conservative performance in Congress one year later, and it seemed obvious (to Liberals) that Hitler's successes accounted for the difference.[49] This interpretation conveniently overlooked Gómez's campaign against the Declaration of Panama, waged several months before the fall of France; but the United States Embassy, among others, tended to share it.[50] Ambassador Braden even began frankly attributing pro-Nazi sympathies to Laureano Gómez—as many of his harsher critics had been doing already—based not only on his Senate remarks and the editorial policy of *El Siglo* but on his observed association with the German and Spanish ministers and other undesirable elements.[51]

The Conservative leader had not made any overt profession of support for the Axis cause; such professions were still generally lacking in Colombia. Indeed the United States still had numerous friends in the Conservative camp, particularly among its elder statesmen. As Braden expressed the matter, with perhaps some slight exaggeration, "upper-class intelligent Conservatives differ with Gómez but the party masses appear to be following him enthusiastically."[52] Those pro-American Conservative oligarchs simply preferred at the moment not to tangle with Laureano and thus kept generally silent all through the middle and latter part of

47. S., Jan. 26, 1941, which comments sarcastically on the inconsistencies of the López faction.

48. *Leyes* (July-Dec., 1941), pp. 31-42.

49. This point was made, e.g., in a long manifesto of the "Liberal majorities" of both houses of Congress at the beginning of the new session in July, 1940 (*L.*, July 24, 1940). What happened later in the session merely strengthened the Liberals' conviction.

50. Braden to Secretary of State, March 26, 1941, DS 821.00/1319.

51. See, e.g., dispatches cited in notes 46 and 50 above, and Braden to Welles, Oct. 9, 1941, DS 821.00/1369.

52. Braden to Secretary of State, Sept. 15, 1940, *FR* (1940), V, 81.

1940 as anti-British and anti-American outbursts became monotonously frequent both in *El Siglo* and in such departmental Conservative organs as *El Deber* of Bucaramanga and *El Figaro* of Cartagena. As the year drew to a close, the air was even filled with rumors of a possible Conservative coup to be carried out with the backing of the European dictatorships,[53] and whether Gómez had really turned Nazi or not, there is no reason to doubt that he would have felt justified in thus following the example of Franco. He was prepared to deal with either side in the world struggle, or with both simultaneously, if he could thereby advance his domestic political objectives. But conditions were not quite as favorable as in Spain, no revolt was attempted, and the precise measure of truth behind the rumors has not been established.

To be sure, the mere fact that such reports were circulating, and could be taken seriously, was one more indication of the continuing impact on Colombia of the German conquest of western Europe. There were likewise assorted hints and suggestions floating about to the effect that the Third Reich would soon be active again as a market for Colombian coffee and a source of needed imports. One rumor of the latter type, duly picked up in the Conservative press, had it that Germany was offering to buy up all Colombia's coffee stocks in return for payment in gold, military equipment, and other merchandise. Supposedly German goods would either be shipped directly across the Atlantic in huge transport planes or else sent by way of Spain or Russia.[54] The moral to be drawn from this sort of thing, obviously, was that Germany was very much a force to be reckoned with—and that Colombia would therefore do well not to tie herself exclusively and irrevocably to the United States.

V

As already indicated, Laureano Gómez and his Conservative legions were not alone in creating difficulties for the Santos administration in the field of foreign policy. Alfonso López was also a problem. López was not fundamentally anti-American, much less pro-Nazi, but he and his adherents were anti-Santos, and they did not treat the conduct of foreign affairs as any kind of privileged sanctuary. Their criticism concerned details of execution more than

53. James H. Wright, Chargé ad interim, to Secretary of State, Oct. 3, 1940, DS 821.00/1297; Braden to Secretary of State, Dec. 19, 1940, DS 821.00/1305.

54. Braden to Secretary of State, June 21, 1940, *FR* (1940), V, 67; *N.Y.T.*, Aug. 16, 1940, 5:3; *El Deber* (Bucaramanga), Oct. 3, 1940.

guiding objectives of policy and therefore differed qualitatively (as well as quantitatively) from that of Gómez. Nevertheless, it seriously troubled the administration, especially as it formed an integral part of a broader struggle for control of the ruling Liberal Party.

For some time *lopista* opposition to Santos's foreign policy was little more than an undercurrent, easily overshadowed by all-out Conservative attacks. It was clearly formulated, and became a central topic of political discussion, only in January, 1941, after López himself returned to Colombia from an extended visit to the United States. The former president then explained his own position in a number of both major and minor addresses, of which the most significant was delivered to a political gathering at the Hotel Granada in Bogotá on January 24. The Hotel Granada speech was not concerned exclusively with foreign policy, but López's remarks on that score attracted a good share of the resulting attention.

In it López sought to claim for himself a sensible middle ground between two extreme positions which he rejected and which he obviously meant to attribute to the Santos administration and the Conservative opposition respectively: "to hand over the fate of Colombia tied to the fate of the United States . . . or to practice a morning gymnastics of suspicion, of rancor, of distrust, of hate."[55] There was no necessary contradiction, he said, between Colombian and United States interests. However, he complained that Colombia, and the Latin American countries generally, had been leaving the initiative to the United States in their mutual relations, with the result that their own needs and viewpoints did not receive adequate consideration. Not only this, but the desirable goal of continental solidarity was being pursued by "eminently dangerous procedures." López explained that by this he meant the Latin American nations were "acquiring very serious and imprecise obligations" on the basis of *ad hoc* decisions hastily arrived at in the face of each new crisis, and in response to each new *fait accompli* of United States policy which was presented to the sister republics for their endorsement.

The latter analysis was remarkably similar to that of Laureano Gómez, but López offered a different solution. Since he rejected a retreat into isolation, he proposed the substitution of a "perma-

55. *L.*, Jan. 25, 1941. Subsequent quotations from, and references to, the Hotel Granada speech are based on this same source.

nent" for an "*ad hoc* jurisprudence" in the field of inter-American security. Ideally this could be done in the form of his own pet idea of an American League of Nations. But one way or another it was necessary to have unambiguous agreements drawn up in advance for dealing, say, with the problem of extra-continental aggression. What constituted such aggression should be unmistakably defined, and the applicable sanctions clearly specified— whether they were to be enforced "jointly or by an explicit delegation." At the same time, López complained that existing *ad hoc* arrangements were heavily weighted on the side of "political solidarity," which was of interest to the United States, as against the "economic cooperation" which would primarily benefit Latin America. Though the United States had promised as far back as the Panama conference that the two would be inseparable and of equal importance, the Latin Americans had not seen to it that the promise was kept.

Turning to the specific case of Colombia, López expressed strong reservations about the recently approved defense-loan project that "does not guarantee defense against the type of attack which is contemplated and which is declared possible as an argument to support its necessity." In effect, it would be quite inadequate to cope with a major threat of aggression; and no such measure should have been adopted without first determining realistically what Colombia's capabilities were and whether there might be other means of defense, "in addition to the purely military," for which external assistance could also be obtained. In this connection, it was the understanding of the United States Embassy that López personally felt Colombia should grant military bases to the United States, instead of pretending to shoulder the main burden of her own defense, and in return get financial compensation that could be used for strengthening the national economy.[56] For political reasons such a course could not be advocated publicly, but López still made clear his belief that the Santos administration was wasting a golden opportunity to bargain for economic aid in its political-military dealings with the United States. He made no reference to the one economic loan already granted to Colombia the previous year by the Export-Import Bank, though he obviously considered it inadequate. He did mention the coffee agreement adopted in November, 1940, by the Latin American producing nations in cooperation with the United States for the purpose of

56. Braden to Secretary of State, Feb. 3, 1941, DS 821.00/1309.

restricting exports and thus supporting the price (which had fallen drastically during the first year of the European war).[57] However, he used it to illustrate the basic inadequacy of Colombian policy, for it was designed only to deal with a passing emergency, whereas Colombia should be vigorously seeking every means to promote diversification and industrial development as long-range solutions to the nation's condition of economic dependence and impoverishment.

The Hotel Granada speech of Alfonso López provoked an immediate counterattack by the administration, whose principal spokesman for the occasion was Finance Minister Carlos Lleras Restrepo. He was the minister who had borne the brunt of López's criticisms, for he was the principal economic and financial adviser to President Santos and had been directly involved in some of the most important Colombian negotiations with the United States. Without going into a detailed defense of political and military cooperation per se, Lleras Restrepo sought to demonstrate that Colombia had in fact obtained an adequate economic *quid pro quo,* citing not only the coffee agreement and the Export-Import Bank loan but also the moral support given by the United States government, over the protest of the Foreign Bondholders Protective Council, to the recent settlement of Colombia's defaulted dollar loans of 1927 and 1928. He also pointed out, reasonably enough, that there was a practical limit to the amount of economic assistance that Colombia could efficiently use at a given moment, or conveniently pay back later.[58]

The López faction, in its turn, sought to demonstrate that the accomplishments listed by Lleras Restrepo were as much—if not more—to the benefit of the United States as to that of Colombia. Coffee stabilization served to restrict the upward as well as downward fluctuation of the market price; the new credits simply went to pay for United States goods; etc., etc.[59] Particularly among the more left-leaning López adherents, there was a discernible anti-American tone to the debate, while the *lopista* attack in general tended to make Santos more fearful than ever of appearing subservient to the United States and thus contributed to the air of indecisiveness often displayed by his administration.[60] However,

57. Below, pp. 83-86.
58. *L.,* Jan. 30, 1941; below, pp. 76-77.
59. See especially *L.,* March 9, 1941, for an analysis by Jorge Zalamea, formerly private secretary to López.
60. Braden to Secretary of State, March 10, 1941, DS 821.00/1317.

the Santos-López argument did not long occupy the center of the stage. Santos could not legally be a candidate to succeed himself for the next presidential term, and no other potential Liberal candidate came close to equaling the popular and political strength of López, which was demonstrated once again by a strong *lopista* showing in the Congressional elections of March, 1941.[61] Once the logic of this situation became sufficiently clear, there was an increasing tendency for Liberals to close ranks at least temporarily in preparation for the coming battle against the Conservative foe—in which Alfonso López was to sally forth as champion of the foreign policy of Eduardo Santos.[62]

VI

Needless to say, the Conservative foe had been an enthusiastic observer of the Liberals' intra-party quarrel. Conservative spokesmen happily pointed out that López was merely repeating criticisms that they had been making all along. They did not, however, welcome him into the fold of right-thinking patriots, because they refused to accept his sincerity. López—"*Símbolo de la Antipatria*" as he was called in the title of one *Siglo* editorial[63]—was the same man who as president had signed a reciprocal trade treaty with the United States that was inimical to Colombian producers, who had been a friend of oil promoters and Wall Street financiers, whose whole past record, in short, made it impossible to take him seriously in his present role as defender of Colombian interests. Conservatives also read into certain statements of López (not primarily those contained in the Hotel Granada speech) a willingness to bargain away what was left of Colombia's neutrality policy, and this was further reason to doubt that he was a true ally in the struggle against United States imperialism.[64] Last but not least, Gómez and other Conservatives had no desire to abet López's drive for re-election. From their standpoint, regardless of whether one took foreign policy into consideration, the Santos brand of Liberalism was a lesser evil.

Nevertheless, the task of commenting on the Liberals' foreign-policy debate provided Conservative spokesmen with many fine opportunities to aim insults of their own in the direction of Wash-

61. *T.*, March 17 and 18, 1941.
62. Below, pp. 114-15, 116.
63. *S.*, March 4, 1941.
64. *La Patria* (Manizales), Jan. 20, 1941; *S.*, Jan. 25 and 26, Feb. 12, and March 13, 1941.

ington. They said little or nothing of substance that they had not said before, but there were still some eyebrow-raising details. For example, there was the interview given by Laureano Gómez to *La Patria* of Manizales, which was also printed in his own newspaper just two days after López's Hotel Granada speech. The headline read: "López Returns to the Country Saturated with the Jewish Propaganda of U.S." The interview actually was not very interesting for what it said about López, but in it Gómez described the United States as now openly a belligerent in the European war and bluntly stated, "In Great Britain, as in the United States, the government is virtually controlled by Semitic elements, which nourish the conflict." Gómez observed that Hitler's work was nothing less than "gigantic" and that his greatest contribution had been the substitution of the "labor standard" for the gold standard, "which constituted the arm of Semitic oppression in the world." The Conservative leader added that there was no point in expressing opinions about the systems of government of the Axis powers— each nation picks the system that suits it best, and democracy would survive even an Axis victory. Indeed there was no danger of Germany establishing world hegemony, no matter what happened in Europe, for Japan and America would both prevent it.[65]

This curious interview revealed Gómez at his worst, as a commentator on world affairs; the general level of discussion in *El Siglo* was not quite as bad. It was still possible to find occasional criticisms of the Axis—or kind words for the United States—in the newspaper. But these were heavily outweighed by the current trend of negative thinking, and one can thus imagine the surprise of habitual readers when they opened the issue of March 23, 1941, and found the lead editorial brimming with Good Neighborliness. Entitled "The Speech of the American Ambassador," it was a laudatory comment on a speech just delivered by Braden on the occasion of an economic fact-finding visit to Colombia by representatives of the National Research Council. The "Américo Latino" column on the same day showed a similar spirit, with friendly treatment even of the latest in the continuing series of high-level military visits exchanged between Colombia and the Canal Zone.[66] The following day "Américo Latino" was almost rhapsodic: "The

65. S., Jan. 26, 1941.
66. S., March 23, 1941. However, this issue still contained an attack on "the imperialism of Saxoamerica" in another article by Francisco José Fandiño Silva.

cause of united America must not perish. On the contrary, today more than ever, such unity is necessary, because on the great clock of human destinies the hour of the supremacy of the new continent has sounded. . . . [It] is the duty of our hemisphere [to follow] the white crest of the great republic of the North and [support] it morally so that it may follow the paths of peace. . . ."[67]

There was an interesting story behind this sudden about-face. For some weeks *El Siglo* had been feeling the financial pinch of a steady withdrawal of advertising for such United States products as Camel cigarettes and Vicks Vapo-Rub. *El Siglo* also learned from the Bogotá agent of its newsprint supplier—which was another American firm—that the agent's New York office had made inquiry about the newspaper's supposed pro-Nazi leanings. At the same time Gómez was aware that there were suspicions held concerning him at the United States Embassy; and apparently he and some of his associates decided it was necessary to take preventive action before a total Yankee quarantine was imposed. The upshot was a meeting on March 20 between Gómez and his close collaborator José de la Vega (co-founder of *El Siglo*) and Braden and one other Embassy official, at the home of a friendly third party. Gómez took the opportunity to offer some complaints about Alfonso López and to remind the Ambassador of López's unfriendly treatment of the United Fruit Company, but the meeting was principally devoted to complaints and denials of allegations in the United States press and elsewhere that he and *El Siglo* were pro-Nazi. He expressed surprise that anyone could consider his Senate speeches anti-American, and he denied having had dealings with the German and Spanish ministers (which was contrary to the observations of the Embassy staff). Braden, on his part, did not try to conceal the fact that he had his doubts about the sincerity of Gómez's friendship, but he did deny that *El Siglo* had been blacklisted by the United States government. He suggested that the loss of advertising was a natural result of patriotic American businessmen reading *El Siglo* and drawing their own conclusions.[68]

The latter explanation was, of course, somewhat disingenuous, since probably few responsible officials of American businesses advertising in *El Siglo* had ever read a copy of it. As a matter of fact, Braden himself had submitted a dispatch to the State Department

67. S., March 24, 1941.
68. Braden to Secretary of State, March 26, 1941, DS 821.00/1319.

the previous August, commenting on the amount of advertising revenue derived by *El Siglo* from United States business sources either through American advertising agencies (which normally liked to have Conservative as well as Liberal press coverage) or through Colombian sales representatives (especially if the latter happened to be Conservatives themselves). He observed that the *lopista* daily *El Liberal* and the weekly *Estampa*, by contrast, seemed to be getting less than their share, despite a friendlier attitude toward the United States. Braden said he was passing this information along just in case United States firms might wish to do something about it;[69] and it would be difficult to document a causal relationship between a dispatch such as this and the cancellations that ultimately occurred. However, it would be most surprising if the Ambassador's views on the matter had no effect at all, especially when he also had excellent personal contacts with the business community. Nor was *El Siglo* the only Conservative organ to suffer loss of American advertising. *La Patria* of Manizales, whose editorial policy was closely similar, had the same difficulty. To some extent, at least, so did even *El Colombiano* of Medellín, the principal mouthpiece of the *antioqueño* Conservative establishment, which had occasionally published anti-American items but could not in any sense be generally classed as anti-American or pro-Nazi.[70] *El Colombiano*, in fact, was one of the few Conservative organs to express misgivings about the Franco regime in Spain, precisely because of the way in which official Hispanism was being allowed to serve as a vehicle for Nazi-Fascist ideological penetration of Latin America.[71]

In any event, the economic pressure of Yankee imperialism was too much for *El Siglo* to withstand. Gómez promised Braden that he would make clear his friendship by changes in editorial policy and, as already indicated, he was as good as his word. Braden was not overly impressed, labeling Gómez a "rice convert," but he felt that good behavior should be rewarded regardless of its motivation and that for the present advertisers might well be encouraged to resume patronage of *El Siglo*. He also found in the episode confirmation of his view that the Conservatives, if they should return to power while international conditions were favorable to the United States, would offer substantially the same co-

---

69. Braden to Secretary of State, Aug. 16, 1940, DS 821.00N/137.
70. Keith to Secretary of State, March 29, 1941, DS 821.00/1322.
71. *El Colombiano* (Medellín), Jan. 10 and 23, 1941.

operation that was being received from the Liberals: plain self-interest, presumably personal as well as national, would see to it.[72]

The effect of the Gómez-Braden discussion, and of *El Siglo*'s difficulties preceding it, did ultimately wear thin and had to be reinforced by new hints or applications of pressure.[73] Moreover, *El Siglo*'s change in attitude was never one hundred per cent. But it was appreciable enough to attract widespread notice, and fortunately it was still in evidence at the time of the German invasion of the Soviet Union in June, 1941. Almost on the eve of the invasion, "Américo Latino" was writing that if war should come to the Western Hemisphere, Latin America would necessarily be on the side of the United States. "Outside of inter-American solidarity and even cooperation," he proclaimed, "there is no salvation."[74] When the attack did occur, there was a strong tendency even for stout anti-Nazis to view the struggle in the East in a very different light from that in the West. President Santos's brother Enrique, who, under the pen name "Calibán" in *El Tiempo*, was the country's leading political columnist, was among the many Colombians who regarded the Soviet Union as, if anything, worse than Nazi Germany and who now expressed a hope that Germany and Russia would conveniently annihilate each other.[75] *El Liberal*, speaking for the López faction, indulged the wishful thought that a victory over Hitler would produce a sharp liberalizing trend within the Soviet Union, but it still noted editorially that "free men of the world" would have difficulty accepting the fact that Russia was now their ally.[76] On balance, it was obvious that Hitler's anti-Soviet crusade

72. Braden to Secretary of State, March 26, 1941, DS 821.00/1319. It was widely understood that *El Siglo* had received some financial assistance from German sources (Fluharty, *Dance of the Millions*, p. 62), but even if Gómez had wished to rely on regular Nazi handouts to make up for the loss of American advertising, this was not really a satisfactory solution. As Braden pointed out, the reputation of being a mere paid propagandist for the Axis would damage his political influence in Colombia; and Hitler could hardly have supplied newsprint if that were also cut off.

73. The extreme case, perhaps, was the temporary rejection of an export permit for newsprint in June, 1942. At just that point, however, the system for controlling newsprint allocations was still being worked out. After September, 1942, specific allocations within Colombia were made by the Colombian government, without United States participation. See *E.*, Dec. 15, 1943, for a copy of *El Siglo*'s rejected application on p. 1, and also Ambassador to Colombia Arthur Bliss Lane to Secretary of State, Dec. 16, 1943, DS 821.00/1640.

74. *S.*, June 16, 1941.

75. *T.*, June 25, 1941. An editorial in the Liberal *El Espectador* expressed essentially the same wish (*E.*, June 23, 1941).

76. *L.*, June 22 and 27, 1941.

had improved his standing even in the Liberal camp,[77] and the same had to be true to a much greater degree among Conservatives.

Under these circumstances the reaction of Gómez and his associates was surprisingly restrained. The first real comment in *El Siglo* came from "Américo Latino," who observed that Hitler's primary motive in attacking Russia was to assure the safety of his rear while later attacking the British Isles and that talk of "liberating Europe and the world from Bolshevism is mere propaganda. . . ." At the same time, he lamented that Communism would derive new respectability from its status as an ally against Hitler, and in later columns he gave his opinion that Communism was ultimately a greater danger than Nazism and that no matter how tawdry Hitler's motives might be, his fight against the Soviets could not help but inspire some degree of support.[78] Nevertheless, *El Siglo*'s qualified backing for Hitler in the East (of which "Américo Latino's" comments were representative) did not automatically bring with it a return to the earlier variety of ranting against Anglo-Saxons. For this result it is probable that the vigilance of Ambassador Braden and the patriotism of Vicks Vapo-Rub executives both deserve some credit.

77. Braden to Secretary of State, July 2, 1941, *FR* (1941), VII, 13-14.
78. S., June 26, 27, and 30, 1941.

Defense and Related Matters

T HE ASSORTED CONTROVERSIES that raged on the subject of Colombian foreign policy, as discussed in the preceding chapter, caused President Santos to weigh his actions carefully in dealing with the United States—often too carefully, in the opinion of United States officials. Yet his excess of caution, in so far as it did in fact exist, concerned methods and timing rather than fundamental policy. In practice, even in the face of domestic criticism, Colombian-United States cooperation proceeded on an ever wider front.

I

In the military sphere the period following the fall of France saw a concerted effort by the United States to multiply and intensify its programs of cooperation with Latin America. In fact even before the final debacle on the western front in Europe, the United States had taken the initiative in proposing special bilateral defense talks with a majority of the Latin American republics, Colombia included. The purpose of the talks would be to determine how far the different countries of the hemisphere were prepared to go in common defense efforts in the light of the changed world situation. A proposal to this effect was presented to the Colombian Foreign Ministry on May 23, 1940; it was formally accepted by President Santos the next day.[1] United States military staff officers then came to Bogotá in June for a preliminary round of conversations with Colombian officers, and they found a cordial reception, but in Colombia as in other Latin American countries the first talks were mainly concerned with establishing principles and identifying problem areas. More detailed provisions were left to be worked out at a second round of staff conversations that took place only after the conclusion of the Havana Conference—in Colombia's case, in September, 1940.[2]

What Colombians of both political parties considered to be their country's primary role in hemispheric defense was, of course, already on record in the pledge of President Santos that no hostile power must be allowed to use Colombian soil in launching an attack on the Panama Canal. And even when, as at Havana, Colombia accepted the doctrine that an extra-continental attack on one American republic was an attack on all, no responsible Colombian official imagined that Colombian military forces would be used to resist such an attack outside their own territory and immediately surrounding waters. This much, at least, was clear from Foreign Minister López de Mesa's otherwise obscure references to "spiritual defense," and certainly the United States had no intention of proposing that Colombian forces serve anywhere away from home. Nevertheless, there were different roles Colombia could play even within her own boundaries, and different degrees of friendly participation that might be allowed the United States. The range of alternatives was great enough to worry Laureano Gómez, and in effect it provided the agenda for the military staff conversations.

When the second round of talks began, on September 10, 1940, the Colombian officers participating once again appeared highly cooperative—so much so that the United States representatives imprudently overlooked the warnings of Ambassador Braden about political nuances and sensitivities. At the close of the first session, they left with the Colombians a draft of a proposed staff agreement containing features Braden had been sure would prove objectionable, and the result was a temporary interruption of the talks. Or, to be more precise, the talks had to be raised temporarily from staff-officer to president-and-ambassador level, with Santos

1. Conn and Fairchild, p. 176; Keith to Secretary of State, May 23 and 24, 1940, *FR* (1940), V, 57-58.
2. Braden to Secretary of State, June 11, 12, 21, and 25, 1940, *FR* (1940), V, 62, 65-70; Conn and Fairchild, pp. 177-78.

objecting, for example, to a reference in the draft to the "recognized" government of Colombia, on the ground that *all* Colombian governments were recognized; to the mention of "fifth column" activity, whose existence in Colombia he denied; and to a provision that Colombia should officially mobilize public support and discourage criticism in case the United States should send armed forces to aid another American republic, on the ground that Colombia could not agree to tamper with freedom of expression.[3]

When the staff talks resumed, they were under close surveillance of both Braden and Colombia's civilian Minister of War, José Joaquín Castro Martínez. They were completed on September 26, without further incident, and produced a series of "Recommendations which the General Staffs . . . Make to their Respective Governments." These were subsequently refined in the course of further discussions between the two governments, and in the process some detailed changes were made. However, everything considered really essential by the United States was agreed to. Colombia emphasized once again that she would endeavor to prevent an attack being made from her territory against that of the United States (specifically including the Canal Zone). At Colombia's request, the United States would help her to resist extra-continental attack; and if the United States should send help to another American nation, as the result of an inter-American decision having Colombia's approval, Colombia would provide facilities to the forces advancing to its aid. Other points that were covered included the lending of technical advisers, adoption of coastal patrol measures, "establishment of adequate channels of communication," and the taking of aerial photographs of Colombian strategic areas, with the unwritten understanding in the latter case that Colombia would provide pilot and aircraft to fly a United States photographer and equipment. In the end, direct mention of aerial photography was deleted at Santos's request, lest the provision give rise to politically inspired attacks. But the unwritten understanding remained, since Santos felt the function itself could perfectly well be carried out under the provision for the lending of technical advisers.[4] The handling of this detail was quite typical of Santos's

3. Braden to Secretary of State, Sept. 13, 1940, *FR* (1940), V, 77-79.
4. Braden to Secretary of State, Sept. 26, 1940, *FR* (1940), V, 82-83; Secretary of State to Braden, Aug. 9, 1941, and Braden to Secretary of State, Sept. 22, 1941, *FR* (1941), VII, 22-24, 27; James H. Wright, Second Secretary of U.S. Embassy, to Secretary of State, Oct. 1, 1940, DS 810.20 Defense /10-140.

tendency to treat defense matters on a personal and informal basis, preferably without setting down on paper anything that might later cause political embarrassment.[5]

It should be noted that some provisions of the staff recommendations were already in effect under the terms of the military mission agreements or other official or unofficial understandings, while still others had to do only with possible action in contingencies that had not yet arisen. It should be noted, too, that despite the rumors of secret base arrangements that kept appearing with regularity,[6] no provision was ever made for the granting of bases on Colombian soil to United States forces. From the start Santos had made clear that as far as he was concerned the task of guarding Colombian territory and waters must remain strictly in the hands of the Colombians themselves (assisted, of course, by United States technical advisers).[7] And even Alfonso López, who apparently favored the granting of bases in return for financial compensations,[8] was careful not to say so in public.

On the other hand, the possibility of the reciprocal use of each other's bases by forces of both countries did come up in confidential discussions. It was casually touched on more than once by Braden and Santos, with varying responses on the part of the latter. It was also strongly favored by Roberto Urdaneta Arbeláez, a Conservative member of the Foreign Ministry's Comisión Asesora, who had served as Foreign Minister himself under Olaya Herrera and was on friendly terms with both the United States Embassy and the Santos administration. Urdaneta was not close to Laureano Gómez—though he later was to serve as acting chief executive under Gómez when the latter finally attained the presidency—but his membership in the opposition party still gave his views a certain strategic importance. Casting himself in the role of a friendly and informal intermediary, Urdaneta proposed to both Braden and Santos that the mutual use of military bases should be worked out through the medium of a general inter-American agreement. However, these rather indirect negotiations came to a head about the time of the German invasion of the Soviet Union, when Santos's fear of public sympathy for the Nazis' anti-Communist crusade undoubtedly added to his normal mood of caution,

5. Braden to Secretary of State, March 28, 1941, *FR* (1941), VII, 3.
6. See, e.g., *N.Y.T.*, March 6, 1940, 10:6, and *L.*, July 24, 1940, citing *Veritas* (Chiquinquirá), for early examples of such rumors.
7. Braden to Secretary of State, June 21, 1940, *FR* (1940), V, 69.
8. Above, p. 42.

and in the end he told Braden that he felt an agreement such as Urdaneta suggested would be politically impossible.[9] Indeed, in his speech to the opening of Congress on July 20, 1941, while as usual dwelling on Colombia's close friendship with the United States, Santos emphasized that the granting of bases had never even been proposed nor did events appear to indicate the need for such a step.[10] The former statement was entirely accurate only if one made a distinction between outright granting and reciprocal use, but it did reflect the political sensitivity of anything that had to do with bases. For the rest, the Santos administration would go in the summer of 1941 only so far as to grant somewhat more liberal flight privileges—informally, of course—to United States military aircraft crossing Colombian territory.[11]

II

One special aspect of military cooperation that was treated in the 1940 staff talks and in many other connections was the furnishing of military equipment to Colombia by the United States. No matter how modest the role Colombia might assume in hemispheric defense, she lacked the equipment to perform it effectively. Most of her war material dated from the mid-1930's or earlier; the Colombian Pacific coast was being patrolled, as of mid-1941, by just one gunboat and two antiquated aircraft; and at one point a United States military adviser predicted that the Colombian Army would run out of ammunition in less than an hour of actual firing.[12] However, the United States, then engaged in its own defense build-up, was in no position to supply all that was thought to be needed. Nor was Colombia in a position to pay for it if it were available.

Despite these practical difficulties, the United States regularly promised to do at least something on Colombia's behalf. The subject of defense equipment received particular attention once the United States set out to invigorate hemispheric defense efforts following the German breakthrough in western Europe. At the

9. Braden to Secretary of State, March 28, May 17, June 25, and July 1, 1941, *FR* (1941), VII, 4-5, 8-9, 11-12. Though he must have heard of López's attitude on the subject of bases, Santos expressed particular concern over the way his Liberal rival might politically exploit a base agreement.

10. *T.*, July 21, 1941.

11. Conn and Fairchild, pp. 261-62.

12. Braden memo, May 27, 1940, *FR* (1940), V, 58-59; Braden to Secretary of State, Jan. 21, 1941, DS 821.00/1308, and July 30, 1941, *FR* (1941), VII, 17.

time of the first-round staff talks in June, 1940, it was discussed directly by President Santos and Ambassador Braden, with the former emphasizing Colombia's needs for aircraft, coast guard cutters, and help in financing their acquisition—although he specified that Colombia would not accept an outright gift of military equipment. A few weeks later, in mid-July, Santos informally suggested that Colombia needed 10 cutters, 60 to 80 aircraft, 50,000 rifles, and still other equipment, whose total cost would come to approximately $16 million. The State Department, in turn, offered cautious encouragement as to the availability of both equipment and financing and urged that Colombia submit a precise list of requirements as quickly as possible.[13]

The list took an inordinately long time to prepare, but meanwhile the Santos administration coaxed through Congress the law of 1940 which authorized it to contract obligations of 30 to 50 million pesos for defense expenditures.[14] Meanwhile, too, military requirements figured largely in the initial negotiations for what became the second Export-Import Bank loan to Colombia, which was finally awarded in July, 1941.[15] Yet in the end that loan was designed to fulfill only economic objectives, since long before Colombia was ready with a proper accounting of military needs, the United States had decided to bring Latin America under the scope of the Lend-Lease Act.[16] Economic and military aid negotiations were henceforth conducted separately.

Early in July, 1941—still without a final statement of requirements from Colombia—the United States presented a draft lend-lease agreement to the Colombian Ambassador in Washington. It authorized the transfer to Colombia of $16.2 million worth of equipment, including $5.5 million in the current fiscal year,[17] but Colombian officials proceeded to raise a number of objections to its terms. Among other things, they disliked the "political flavor" of certain statements contained in it—meaning, in effect, some generalities about hemisphere defense embedded in the preamble—and complained that it was designed to provide only equipment, whereas additional funds would be needed for Colombia to make the best use of the equipment. In the latter case, Ambassador Bra-

13. Braden to Secretary of State, June 11 and 21, and July 10, 1940, and Secretary of State to Braden, July 13, 1940, *FR* (1940), V, 63, 68, 71-74.
14. Above, pp. 37, 38-39.
15. Below, pp. 78-79.
16. Conn and Fairchild, pp. 215, 221-24.
17. Welles to Braden, July 9, 1941, *FR* (1941), VII, 15.

den saw some merit in the Colombian position, pointing to the example of steel houses which the War Ministry had bought in the United States two years earlier and which were still stored at Barranquilla for lack of money to take them out and erect them at strategic points. However, such "free" funds could not be supplied under existing lend-lease legislation, and officials in Washington, having reluctantly acquiesced in a steady escalation of Colombian demands for economic assistance during negotiations for the latest Export-Import Bank loan, were unreceptive to the idea of a new loan just now for defense purposes. At one point Santos proposed to abandon the lend-lease procedure entirely in favor of a straight loan of $6 million, which Colombia might use to cover her immediate equipment needs through outright purchase and still have funds left over for related expenditures, but an arrangement of this sort was ruled out both by Washington's present disinclination to extend another monetary loan and by the fact that the equipment itself could be sent more expeditiously under lend-lease auspices.[18]

The figure Santos cited of $6 million for the proposed loan was another indication of the prevailing confusion as to the exact amount of Colombian requirements for equipment and funds for military purposes. The $16.2 million specified in the lend-lease draft was roughly the figure informally mentioned by Santos for equipment needs in July, 1940, but most later discussions revolved about substantially lesser—though widely varying—sums. Ambassador Braden, on his part, had decided reservations as to how much equipment Colombia could efficiently use and even remarked to Colombian officials that perhaps they should be thinking in terms of hundreds of thousands, not millions, of dollars for defense expenditures.[19] Nevertheless, he favored granting military aid in one form or other not only for the minimal contribution Colombia could make with it to the defense of the hemisphere but also for the sake of Colombian domestic tranquillity. For one thing, he felt that new equipment would help to keep the armed forces happy and out of mischief. Much the same point was made by President Santos in support of the need for "free" funds when he emphasized that the discontent of troops and noncommissioned officers

18. Braden to Secretary of State, July 30 and Sept. 19, 1941, and Secretary of State to Braden, Aug. 5 and Sept. 25, 1941, FR (1941), VII, 17-18, 20-21, 26, 28-30.
19. Braden to Secretary of State, Oct. 28, 1940, DS 821.51/2553, Sept. 26, Oct. 3, and Dec. 15, 1941, FR (1941), VII, 30-31, 34, 36-37.

with shabby uniforms and barracks was a factor played upon by the organizers of a minor conspiracy suppressed in August, 1941. Nor, finally, did it make sense for the United States to continue training Colombian personnel in the use of modern equipment which they either did not have or did not have enough of. At the very least, such a course was bound to generate new frustrations.[20]

A final objection to the proposed lend-lease arrangements was raised by Santos in October, 1941, when he informed Braden that the law passed by Congress the year before to authorize borrowing for defense would not cover a transaction of this sort and that new legislation was needed. From that point until after Pearl Harbor, lend-lease discussions appear to have languished, to be revived only in the new situation created by the full-scale entry of the United States into the war.[21] A lend-lease agreement was actually signed on March 17, 1942.[22] Even before that, however, the United States had been making efforts to provide military equipment to Colombia on at least a limited scale. It was hampered in doing so, not merely by the Colombians' difficulty in deciding what they wanted and on what terms, but also, very definitely, by the lack of any large exportable surplus at this stage in the United States. Training planes, for example, were promised as a natural complement to the work of the aviation mission; and their slowness in arriving was an evident source of irritation to the Colombians.[23]

III

Closely related to military cooperation per se—particularly in the view of United States observers—was cooperation for the prevention of espionage and of "fifth column" activities generally. In this broad area the two governments shared similar objectives and were committed to the principle of collaboration, but United States officials normally took a more serious view of the dangers present in Colombia than did their Colombian counterparts. They were sometimes unnecessarily alarmist, as when Ambassador Braden made the offhand estimate that 60 per cent to 80 per cent of Colombian army officers had Nazi sympathies.[24] This was without

20. Braden to Secretary of State, Aug. 14 and Sept. 26, 1941, *FR* (1941), VII, 25, 32; on the conspiracy referred to, see *T.*, Aug. 5, 1941.
21. Braden to Secretary of State, Oct. 3 and Dec. 15, 1941, *FR* (1941), VII, 33-35.
22. Below, pp. 108-9.
23. See Braden to Secretary of State, July 30, 1941, *FR* (1941), VII, 18.
24. Braden to Welles, Oct. 9, 1941, DS 821.00/1369.

any doubt an excessive figure, unless he was referring mainly to their professional admiration for the prowess of the German army. The United States did, however, have more and better information on potential fifth columnists than did the Colombian government itself, most notably some extensive files on members of the local German colony[25]—which at the time of Pearl Harbor numbered somewhat over 4,000 persons.[26] From this information it was evident that in addition to, and really overlapping with, the German diplomatic-consular and commercial organizations in Colombia there was also a Nazi political organization whose "Fuehrer" was the Barranquilla businessman Emil Pruefert.[27] Backing up the Germans themselves was a fringe of Colombian sympathizers and collaborators and related groups of Italians, Japanese, and, especially in the propaganda field, pro-Franco Spaniards.

Propaganda was far and away the most obvious output of this network of Axis subjects and sympathizers. German firms such as Bayer used advertising funds to promote Axis propaganda in the Colombian press and airwaves, just as American firms used the threat of loss of advertising to combat it. The United States, fortunately, had much the largest advertising budgets to work with, but there were other ways of spreading the news of Nazi superiority. In addition, Germans for one reason or another had done a good bit of mapping, photographing of bridges, and so forth.[28] They were even alleged to have such refinements as a secret chemical warfare unit in readiness on Colombian soil,[29] while their Axis

25. Braden to Secretary of State, July 6, 1940, DS 821.00N/93.
26. *L.*, Dec. 19, 1941.
27. Consul Nelson R. Park, Barranquilla, to Secretary of State, June 21, 1940, DS 821.00N/79; Braden to Secretary of State, July 6, 1940, DS 821.00N /93, and Dec. 19, 1940, DS 821.00/1305; *N.Y.T.*, Aug. 19, 1940, 34:1; William N. Simonson, "Nazi Infiltration in South America, 1933-1945" (doctoral dissertation, Fletcher School of Law and Diplomacy, 1964), pp. 257-59, 269-72, 299-300, 312, 408-9. Pruefert's official title was "Landesgruppenleiter Kolumbien" (cf. Germany, Auswärtiges Amt, "Records of . . . Received by the Department of State," roll 103, frame 110890). Only a random sample of the captured German documents of Latin American interest that are available on microfilm was consulted in the preparation of this study; however, the author was struck by the relative scarcity of items from or references to Colombia.
28. See, e.g., Vice-Consul Vernon L. Fluharty, "Memorandum of Subversive Activities and the General Political Situation . . ." Medellín, May 7, 1942, DS 821.00/1414.
29. *N.Y.T.*, Aug. 18, 1940, 16:1. Simonson, in his discussion of the Nazis' underground para-military apparatus—which he concluded to have been unusually well-developed in Colombia—reproduces an extremely elaborate table

associates had a "notorious Japanese bean field" near Cali which was guarded by an electrified fence and was thought to shelter much suspicious equipment.[30]

Even if one granted that there was considerable truth as well as some exaggeration in what was said about Axis activities in Colombia, there was room for valid disagreement as to the significance of it all. President Santos, who refused to become alarmed on this score, generally denied that anything that could properly be called a fifth column existed in Colombia; he admitted concern about Axis propaganda, but the rest he apparently dismissed either as imaginary or as constituting no real danger.[31] War Minister Castro Martínez was less confident,[32] and the right-wing Liberal daily *La Razón* (whose managing editor was an anti-Nazi Spaniard) made almost a specialty of alerting Colombians to the peril within.[33] But most other newspapers, Liberal as well as Conservative, either ridiculed the peril or were restrained in their treatment of it, and they easily took offense at alarmist reports published in the United States. "Frankly all that is not very serious [*poco serio*] and somewhat offensive," was the way *El Tiempo* referred to one series of exposés on the fifth-column danger in Colombia that appeared in the *New York Times* during August, 1940.[34] *El Liberal*, though less complacent than *El Tiempo*, referred to the same type of reporting as one of the principal threats to good United States-Colombian relations.[35] Foreign Minister López de Mesa was still another who expressed displeasure: he once mentioned to Ambassador Braden his fear that the United States might be misled by press reports of Nazi penetration into relying less on Colombian cooperation and even into taking hasty unilateral action. To which Braden wisely replied that if the American people were convinced there was no Nazi danger in Colombia it might be harder

---

of organization for Colombia in which the chemical warfare unit is shown ("Nazi Infiltration," pp. 269-72). Precisely what it consisted of in practice, however, has not been established.

30. Braden to Secretary of State, Jan. 21, 1941, DS 821.00/1308, and March 21, 1941, DS 821.001 López/125.

31. Braden to Secretary of State, June 11, 1940, *FR* (1940), V, 62; cf. above, p. 34.

32. Braden to Secretary of State, June 12, 1940, *FR* (1940), V, 65.

33. Keith to Secretary of State, June 7, 1940, DS 821.00N/71; cf. *R.*, May 23-29 and 31, 1940.

34. *T.*, Aug. 23, 1940; *N.Y.T.*, Aug. 15, 1940, 6:3, Aug. 16, 1940, 5:3, Aug. 17, 1940, 7:6, Aug. 18, 1940, 16:1, Aug. 19, 1940, 34:1.

35. *L.*, Nov. 21, 1941.

to obtain financial assistance for purposes of Colombian defense.[36]

Despite its more relaxed attitude, the Colombian government was not unwilling to cooperate in heading off internal Axis threats: its role in the SCADTA affair is a case in point. It also adopted a number of measures for the general control of foreign residents, which in practice were directed chiefly at the German colony such as the decree of June 25, 1940, that among other things firmly prohibited any form of propagandizing on behalf of "foreign political organizations." This decree, which Braden praised as a prompt and constructive response to the situation created by the fall of France, was drafted by the Secretary General of the Foreign Ministry immediately following a luncheon discussion of the problem of subversive activities with a member of the Embassy staff.[37] From time to time a few Germans would be arrested by the Colombian authorities on charges of illicit propaganda, suspected espionage, or something comparable.[38] And, finally, the Colombian government made some efforts, with United States assistance, to improve its intelligence services. These, however, continued to lack sufficient money, manpower, and technical equipment, and did not inspire complete confidence. Certainly the exchange of intelligence data with the United States was essentially one way: as of December, 1940, the Embassy in Bogotá estimated that 85 per cent of the material in Colombian intelligence files came from United States sources, 10 per cent from Colombian sources, and 1 per cent from the British legation. The remainder was regarded as worthless, with no indication of origin, though it is quite possible that part of the 85 per cent was worthless too.[39]

Be that as it may, the problem of real or alleged fifth-column activities came briefly to the very forefront of Colombian-United States relations when President Roosevelt, in a radio broadcast on September 11, 1941, casually referred to the existence of a secret German airfield in Colombia.[40] The resulting petty crisis nicely illustrated both the ambiguities inherent in the problem and its potential as an irritant. Roosevelt did not spell out all the details in his speech, but it was soon apparent that the installation to

36. Braden to Secretary of State, Sept. 3, 1940, DS 711.21/950.

37. *MemRels* (1940), pp. 58-61; Braden to Secretary of State, June 26, 1940, DS 821.00N/85.

38. See, e.g., *N.Y.T.*, Dec. 23, 1940, 11:2, and Jan. 3, 1941, 6:5.

39. Braden to Secretary of State, July 6, 1940, DS 821.00N/93, and Dec. 19, 1940, DS 821.00/1305.

40. *N.Y.T.*, Sept. 12, 1941, 1:8, and Sept. 13, 1941, 6:6.

which he referred was one supposedly located on the country estate of Dr. Hans Neumueller, a well-established German resident of Cartagena. While there was certainly no full-scale aerodrome (secret or otherwise) on Neumueller's property, it did include at least one stretch where airplanes could in fact have landed.[41] Not much else is clear.

Inevitably Roosevelt's statement set off a wave of excitement in Colombia. The War Ministry seemed to confirm the report when it revealed that the government had received information of the "probable" existence of secret airfields and reassured the public that it was quite capable of controlling the situation. Adding to the confusion, Foreign Minister López de Mesa informed Congress that such charges had been made for several years but that the government on the basis of its own investigations had been unable to confirm them. The Colombian Senate then proceeded, by unanimous vote and even with some indignation, to proclaim its own conviction that no secret airfields existed—that Roosevelt was mistaken. This inspired *El Liberal* to ask editorially how, if the airfields were secret, the Senate could be so sure none existed; and just to play safe, the Liberal-dominated (though Communist-infiltrated) Confederación de Trabajadores de Colombia publicly asked for the expulsion of Neumueller from Colombia.[42]

But Conservatives made the greatest use of the airfield incident. The moderate and generally pro-American *El Colombiano* of Medellín contented itself chiefly with criticizing Colombian official spokesmen for the vague and contradictory nature of their statements.[43] On the other hand, *La Patria* of Manizales, whose reaction essentially typified that of the hard-line rightist element, found an excellent opportunity to attack both the Santos administration and Franklin D. Roosevelt: "It is not true that the landing fields exist? Well then, the President of the United States has slandered Colombia. And one could argue: with what object? To the simplest the answer occurs: in order to invade us. Thus it is that in Colombia there exist secret Nazi landing fields, and that 'General' Castro Martínez puts down a Nazi conspiracy every two weeks, for then

41. Braden to Secretary of State, Oct. 18, 1941, DS 740.00112A EW1939/3198.
42. *L.*, Sept. 12 and 13, 1941; *N.Y.T.*, Sept. 16, 1941, 8:4.
43. *El Colombiano,* Sept. 14, 1941. The previous day it had offered a generally laudatory commentary on Roosevelt's speech, without making reference to the airfield charge.

there is sufficient cause to occupy the dangerous territory."[44] That such fears were easily kindled was made evident later the same month when a rumor suddenly spread in Bogotá—even broadcast over the radio, but immediately denied—that United States Marines had already landed at various points of the Colombian coast.[45]

IV

One major aspect of the campaign against Axis propagandists and potential fifth columnists was the use of economic pressure either to diminish the resources at their disposal or otherwise to deter certain types of activity. Two notable examples of such pressure have already been examined: the use of Pan American's controlling financial interest as a lever for the de-Germanization of SCADTA and the use of American advertising funds to moderate the opinions of El Siglo. These, of course, were somewhat special cases, but the purging of SCADTA employees had a close parallel in the decision of other United States business firms to fire employees or sales representatives in Colombia—above all if they were Axis nationals—who might be tempted to use their positions to advance objectives inimical to the United States. Firms that did not do so rapidly enough were subject (as Pan American had been) to official prodding, e.g., from the Embassy in Bogotá.[46]

As the case of El Siglo demonstrated, even individuals and enterprises not directly linked to American firms might be subjected to United States pressure. If it appeared that to do business with them would be contrary to United States and hemispheric interests, American citizens could be informally advised to take their business elsewhere. Such casual blacklisting was institutionalized in July, 1941, when the United States published its Proclaimed List of suspected Axis agents or sympathizers with whom American firms and private citizens were forbidden to do business.[47] At that time controls and shortages resulting from the defense build-up in the United States meant that inclusion on the Proclaimed List was a definite handicap, complicating the task of obtaining many

44. *La Patria*, Sept. 13, 1941.
45. *El Colombiano*, Sept. 28, 1941; *N.Y.T.*, Sept. 29, 1941, 3:7.
46. Braden was particularly annoyed at the employment by the Associated Press of a German national in Bogotá who also worked for the Nazi Transocean agency; he was still employed even after the fall of France, and after the Embassy had made a special effort to have him dismissed (Braden to Secretary of State, July 29, 1940, DS 821.00N/118).
47. David L. Gordon and Royden Dangerfield, *The Hidden Weapon: The Story of Economic Warfare* (New York, 1947), pp. 152-53.

scarce articles, and the fact that New York banks commonly served as clearing centers even for financial transactions between Colombia and other Latin American countries gave further scope to the system's operation. Since it was designed ostensibly to control the dealings of American citizens, not foreigners, the Proclaimed List was administered in Washington, unilaterally; but it obviously affected foreigners, and not just those who were formally blacklisted. Firms not on the list were understandably wary of dealing with those that were, for fear that they might also be included.

Firms operating in Colombia were included on the Proclaimed List from the very beginning, and their number subsequently grew[48] despite the fact that some were deleted from time to time either because of a change in their policies and practices or because adverse political repercussions of their inclusion outweighed the possible benefits. In some cases the deletion of native Colombian firms was sought by the Colombian government itself, which also requested assurances that Colombian firms would be placed on the list only on the basis of clear and effective danger and only after careful coordination with it. But the United States, though never averse to a reasonable amount of consultation, had no intention of surrendering its own right of ultimate decision; and neither did President Santos care to make a major issue of the Proclaimed List.[49]

Nevertheless, there was widespread annoyance with the system in Colombia, and *El Siglo* predictably was among those annoyed. Yet it approached the issue with a degree of caution that no doubt reflected among other things its own desire not to be placed on the list. In one editorial dealing with the Proclaimed List, which appeared under the title "Complex of Timidity," the Conservative organ was almost effusive in its praise of the Good Neighbor Policy—emphatically denying the existence in the United States of the "imperialist tendency" that it had once talked so much about— and took a generally understanding view of the United States position on the question of blacklisting. It admitted to "kindred

48. See, e.g., *L.*, Sept. 26, 1941. By mid-1942 over 400 firms and individuals operating in Colombia were on the U.S. Proclaimed List (*MemHda* [1942], p. 24).

49. *T.*, Oct. 10 and 11, 1941. The Foreign Ministry, and in particular Foreign Minister López de Mesa, was more inclined than Santos himself to press for changes in Proclaimed List procedures. In this connection, López de Mesa gave at least tacit approval to the protest resolution of the Colombian Senate discussed below (Braden to Secretary of State, Nov. 13, 1941, DS 740.00112A EW1939/3365).

interests in danger, which demand an elemental solidarity for the common defense." But the same editorial detected in the application of the Proclaimed List a tendency to punish "innocent attitudes or sympathies" of Colombian citizens who did not constitute a real threat to anyone, and it took the Santos administration severely to task for failing, as the title suggested, to stand up boldly for the Colombians in question.[50]

That criticism of the Proclaimed List was not a strictly partisan matter was made clear by the unanimous adoption by the Colombian Senate of a resolution demanding that Latin American firms or individuals be included on it only after due consultation with their respective governments, "in accord with the spirit and the letter of the acts and conventions of solidarity subscribed at Lima, Panama, and Havana."[51] This resolution, passed in November, 1941, had been presented to the Senate by a special committee named to study the problem, whose full report was even more strongly worded and was also approved unanimously. The committee membership was drawn from both parties and included José de la Vega of El Siglo's official hierarchy, who was particularly indignant over the blacklisting of Laboratorios Román in his native Cartagena; though he felt the report was still too mild, he went along with it, he said, to make a show of national unity.

According to the Senate committee, the "system of blacklists" was contrary to both general international law and the concept of inter-American reciprocity. In its "practical aspect," moreover, it was "completely inadmissible. In effect, to form such lists the diplomatic and consular agents of the belligerent State [i.e., the United States] have to organize a true service of espionage, incompatible with their normal functions and contrary to the sovereignty of the country where they reside. . . ." The committee then explained the scope of the consultation which it felt necessary: "Our fellow nationals, even those who for reasons of internal politics are estranged from the present administration, would feel secure in their rights if the subterranean denunciations—almost always the work of mischievous passions or commercial competition—of having connections with foreign powers were submitted to the judgment [dictamen] of the President of the Republic or of his Minister of Foreign Relations, before receiving the sentence of condemnation of a foreign power."[52] The United States did not

50. S., Oct. 11, 1941. See also S., Nov. 2, 1941.
51. S., Nov. 8, 1941.   52. Ibid.

proceed to do what the Colombian Senate asked, and Santos himself refused to circulate the Senate resolution to the other American governments as called for by its terms.[53] But it is perhaps safe to assume that the strength and unanimity of feeling expressed by the resolution were taken into account in administering the Proclaimed List in relation to Colombian firms.

V

The Proclaimed List was only one of various regulatory mechanisms, adopted by the United States as it increasingly entered a war economy, that had a direct impact upon the trade and economic life of Colombia. Export controls in the United States, for example, not only cut off scarce supplies entirely from blacklisted firms but also limited the amounts available to Colombian businessmen whose political leanings were beyond suspicion. There was at least an element of bilateralism in the operation of such controls, since Colombia supplied both general information on national requirements to guide planners in Washington and specific official recommendations as required for the issuance of certain types of permits. Colombia likewise cooperated to the extent of imposing controls on the re-export, from her own territory, of articles subject to export control in the United States.[54]

Still another aspect of economic collaboration was the marshaling of Colombian material resources in support of the United States defense effort. Colombia was not a major supplier of strategic materials, but she did have a contribution to make and her potential as a source of platinum—of which she was the principal Latin American producer—gave rise to intensive negotiations with the United States starting in the first half of 1941. The article was of special importance not only because it was needed in the United States but because it was equally desirable to keep it from falling into the hands of the Axis powers. Japan, in particular, had been an active buyer of Colombian platinum.

In May, 1941, accordingly, the State Department relayed to Bogotá an offer of the Metals Reserve Company, an agency of the Reconstruction Finance Corporation, to buy up the entire Colombian output of platinum less whatever was now being shipped commercially to private buyers in the United States. President

53. Braden to Secretary of State, Nov. 14, 1941, *FR* (1941), VI, 305-6, and Nov. 21, 1941, DS 740.00112A EW1939/3944.
54. *MemEcNac* (1942), p. 39; *MemRels* (1942), p. 165.

Santos promptly gave an enthusiastic response, but before the transaction was finally closed certain complications had to be overcome. There were legal technicalities in Colombia, although none was insuperable. There was also a natural desire on Colombia's part to use the platinum question for bargaining purposes in extracting commitments for the delivery of needed imports. Above all, Colombia wanted a guaranteed supply of silk, which was required for five small textile factories. She had been dependent on Japan for the article in question, but the Japanese were not interested in continuing to sell silk unless they in turn could obtain Colombian platinum. A United States offer to supply rayon instead was not wholly satisfactory, since it would take time to convert the local factories to handle it.

Finally, there was disagreement about the price. The Metals Reserve Company first suggested $36 an ounce, which was more than the American-owned South American Gold and Platinum Company was charging for the Colombian platinum it sold in the United States but less than Colombian producers had been receiving from other countries, and not enough to discourage contraband sales to Japan or elsewhere. Thus in the end a higher figure was accepted, and Colombia also settled, in effect, for mere assurances that the United States would do the best it could to keep Colombian factories supplied with raw material. Final arrangements were not signed until February, 1942, but long before that the United States proposal had been accepted in principle; and steps had been taken to halt Japanese purchases even before Pearl Harbor.[55]

55. Select documents on the platinum negotiations are contained in *FR* (1941), VII, 40-55. See also *MemHda* (1942), pp. 44-45, and *Decretos de carácter extraordinario expedidos por el Organo Ejecutivo en desarrollo de las facultades conferidas por las Leyes 128 y 152 de 1941* (Bogotá, 1942), pp. 41-42.

Loans Old and New

RUNNING THROUGH all discussions of Colombian-United States political solidarity and military cooperation was an undercurrent—sometimes frankly acknowledged, at other times tacitly understood—of financial considerations. No price in dollars or pesos was set on the friendship of either country, but each had certain financial interests for which it expected sympathetic treatment from the other. This meant, in the case of Colombia, that if the Santos administration loyally sided with the United States in international affairs it naturally expected financial as well as military assistance in return, to enable it to withstand the impact of the world crisis. From the standpoint of the United States, moreover, it went without saying that any full understanding between the two countries ought to include some settlement of the Colombian dollar loans which had been in default since the years of the great depression. Indeed the most important single item of unfinished business in United States-Colombian relations at the start of the Santos administration was the adjustment of Colombia's defaulted obligations. President Santos had barely taken office in August, 1938, when he received a telegram from President Francis White of the Foreign Bondholders Protective Council (FBPC) in New York calling his attention specifically to this matter; and though the official Colombian reply was a mere promise to study the debt question, both Santos and Minister of Finance Carlos Lleras Restrepo were genuinely anxious to reach an agreement.[1]

The question was inherently complex, since several different classes of obligations were involved, with a grand total (not counting arrears of interest) of around $170 million.[2] First and foremost there was the unpaid balance of two 6 per cent bond issues floated in the United States by the Colombian national government in 1927 and 1928, for $25 million and $35 million respectively. Full service had been maintained on these until 1932, when amortization of principal was suspended but the required interest was still paid in cash. Then, in 1933, Colombia met the interest charges by paying partly in cash and partly in non-interest-bearing scrip. In 1934 interest was paid wholly in 4 per cent funding certificates; and after January 1, 1935, default became complete on both loans. However, the scrip issued in 1933 was redeemed at maturity in 1937, and service (including gradual retirement) was likewise maintained on the certificates which had been issued the following year. For that matter, the principal of the original loans had been reduced to slightly over $51 million by the time regular amortization was discontinued, and another $6 million worth of the bonds had come into the hands of the Colombian government itself in exchange for internal bonds, so that the actual amount of principal still owed was now between $45 million and $46 million.[3]

Apart from this bonded indebtedness, Colombia owed a smaller balance resulting from a loan made to the Olaya Herrera administration during its first year in office by a consortium of the National City Bank of New York and other banking institutions. The loan had been made, supposedly, on a short-term basis, to tide Colombia over until more long-term credits could be obtained, but in practice no such credits were ever forthcoming, and the loan had therefore been repeatedly renewed—always for short periods—ever since. Interest on this "banking group loan" had been maintained, but at

1. *MemHda* (1940), p. 139.
2. Institute of International Finance, *Republic of Colombia* (Bulletin no. 98, March 7, 1938), pp. 21-24. The figures given in this source are as of June 30, 1937, but the size of indebtedness had not changed significantly by the start of the Santos administration. It should be noted that the approximate total mentioned in the text does not take account of a miscellaneous assortment of sterling loans, the oldest going back to 1906, or of dollar debts owed to private business firms for construction activities and the like.
3. *MemHda* (1932), pp. 39-44; *MemHda* (1940), pp. 136-37; *MemHda* (1941), p. 27; *N.Y.T.*, Dec. 31, 1940, 26:1.

a reduced rate arranged by agreement with the lenders, and some redemption of principal had also been carried out, though without any fixed plan. By 1938 the balance stood in the neighborhood of $15 million. In this case, Colombia was not exactly in default, but the loan had obviously turned into something different from what was originally intended, and the bankers were anxious to make definite arrangements for its liquidation as soon as possible.[4]

Finally, there were still other obligations at stake that did not involve the Colombian national government as immediate borrower. During the 1920's Colombian departments and municipalities had issued an even larger sum in dollar bonds, on which payments were suspended in the depression, leaving approximately $82 million in principal still outstanding.[5] Additional dollar bonds had been issued during the same period by various official and private lending institutions in Colombia, of which the most important was the Banco Agrícola Hipotecario (i.e., Agricultural Mortgage Bank). The issues of the latter, which was an official agency, had been expressly guaranteed by the Colombian treasury, but they had been in complete default since 1935. The obligations of the private institutions—Banco de Colombia, Banco Hipotecario de Colombia, and Banco Hipotecario de Bogotá—did not have such a guarantee and had been in default since 1932. But even in their case the credit of the Colombian government was involved as a result of legislation enacted in the depression emergency which transferred responsibility for their foreign obligations to the Banco Agrícola Hipotecario. The combined principal still outstanding of both guaranteed and nonguaranteed issues was something over $20 million, although a substantial part of this amount was actually in the hands of the bank itself.[6]

In practice it was the national dollar loans of 1927 and 1928 that chiefly engaged the attention of the Colombian government, the United States financial community, and (as a benevolently interested third party) the Department of State. Not only was the default on those two issues the most damaging to Colombian for-

---

4. *Colombia Yearbook*, VII, 207 (New York, 1935); *MemHda* (1940), p. 155. On the circumstances surrounding the granting of the banking group loan, see *FR* (1931), II, 28-37.

5. Institute of International Finance, *Colombia* (Bulletin no. 53, July 8, 1932), pp. 17-33, and *Republic of Colombia* (Bulletin no. 98), p. 24.

6. Institute of International Finance, *Colombia* (Bulletin no. 53), pp. 33-35, and *Republic of Colombia* (Bulletin no. 98), p. 24; *L.*, June 25, 1942; Frederick Livesey, memo, March 6, 1942, *FR* (1942), VI, 213.

eign credit, but any settlement made concerning them could be expected to set a pattern for the handling of other obligations. During the preceding López administration, Colombia had already negotiated somewhat fitfully with bondholders' representatives for a resumption of interest and amortization, but the chief Colombian offer had featured a reduction of interest to 2 per cent, increasing annually by one quarter of one per cent until a maximum of 3 per cent was reached. Such a settlement was considered wholly unacceptable by the FBPC. The Santos administration hoped to revive the negotiations, but it moved slowly because it did not wish to overcommit its resources and because any settlement that appeared too generous to foreign creditors could easily become a domestic political liability. There was in fact widespread sentiment in the Colombian Congress in favor of making a unilateral offer to the bondholders, on Colombia's own terms and as a take-it-or-leave-it proposition. Legislation to that effect was averted, apparently thanks to administration pressure, but the first approach taken by Finance Minister Lleras Restrepo was still simply to gather additional data which might be used to convince the FBPC that the rejected López offer was the most Colombia could afford.[7]

In the end, probably the one factor that did most to induce Colombia to improve her offer was the hope of obtaining new credits from the United States once the old ones were settled to mutual satisfaction. The two questions—old loans and new loans—were deftly interwoven by Ambassador Braden in talks with both Santos and Lleras Restrepo soon after he assumed his duties in Bogotá early in 1939. Citing instructions he had received from President Roosevelt to discuss the problem of currency stabilization, Braden mentioned to Santos during an interview on February 22 that if Colombia so desired the United States might be willing to make a treasury-to-treasury loan of gold bullion for stabilization purposes. Santos replied with a polite expression of interest and with the observation that Colombia's problem, for the moment, was to prevent an undue appreciation, not depreciation, of the peso. However, once the possibility of new credits had been raised, Braden on his part made clear that the settlement of defaulted past obligations would have a direct bearing on a stabilization loan or any other kind of economic cooperation. In this connection he was careful to emphasize the political influence within the United

7. Braden to Secretary of State, May 15, 1939, FR (1939), V, 469-72.

States of the community of foreign bondholders, as he was to do again on numerous similar occasions.[8]

A more detailed discussion of the loan question, in both aspects, took place some weeks later between Braden and Lleras Restrepo, who enjoyed unusual independence in his capacity as Finance Minister both because of the implicit trust that Santos had in him and because of Santos's recognition of his own lack of expert knowledge in the field.[9] With regard to past debts, Lleras pressed the Ambassador to express an opinion on the specific terms that should be offered, and Braden said frankly that he felt those put forward by the López administration were too low. He gave as his personal opinion that Colombia easily could and should offer 3 per cent interest to begin with, to be scaled upward as national revenues permitted. Lleras also dwelt at length on the need for future credits, expressing somewhat more interest than Santos in the possibility of a currency stabilization loan and specifying a number of other worthy objectives for which he hoped Colombia might obtain financing through the Export-Import Bank. Among those he mentioned were railway construction and acquisition of rolling stock, machinery for roadbuilding and for Magdalena River dredging, and addition to the capital of the Caja de Crédito Agrario, Industrial y Minero. And just as the United States Ambassador held out the hope of new loans while urging the settlement of old, the Colombian Finance Minister held out hope that with an infusion of official credits from Washington Colombia might be in a better position to dismantle her present exchange-control system, which was highly distasteful on both practical and theoretical grounds to the United States.[10]

Despite Braden's expressed opinion that the terms previously offered were too low, the Colombian government made one more effort to obtain their acceptance by the FBPC. Naturally the effort failed. It may not even have been a serious attempt, for according to the general view in Bogotá, as reported by Braden, Colombia was simply trying to elicit a counterproposal.[11] However, when

8. Braden to Secretary of State, March 3, 1939, DS 711.21/931. Braden appears to have been careful not to state categorically that a debt settlement must precede the granting of new credits; as he indicated in the meeting with Lleras Restrepo discussed in the following paragraph, a settlement would simply have to be fairly well assured.

9. Braden to Secretary of State, July 18, 1939, *FR* (1939), V, 492.

10. Braden to Secretary of State, May 15, 1939, *FR* (1939), V, 472-81.

11. Secretary of State to Braden, July 1, 1939, *FR* (1939), V, 481; Braden to Secretary of State, July 13, 1939, *FR* (1939), V, 487.

White of the FBPC proceeded to raise the possibility of a temporary one-year agreement to resume interest at 3 per cent, Lleras was unenthusiastic; and when the FBPC suggested further that a permanent settlement be worked out on the basis of 3.5 per cent interest, gradually rising to 4.5 per cent, Colombia was again unreceptive. By the end of July, 1939, negotiations appeared to have broken down almost entirely.[12]

With the outbreak of war in Europe, the situation changed again. Because well over half of her foreign trade was conducted with the United States, Colombia enjoyed some degree of protection against immediate adverse effects of the European struggle on her economy; but she could not escape its impact entirely. Above all, the disruption of established European trade patterns led to a sharp drop in the market price of coffee, which in Colombia's case fell by more than one-third from September, 1939, to May, 1940.[13] This blow, combined with such other factors as a great spurt in imports ordered during 1939 in anticipation of the war's outbreak, caused Colombia to end that year with a balance-of-payments deficit of more than $8 million; for just the first half of 1940 the figure was $11.6 million.[14] To cope with the exchange situation, Colombia tightened exchange control regulations,[15] but there was a corollary problem in that around 40 per cent of the national government's revenue was derived from levies on foreign trade:[16] thus, to the extent that imports were cut back in line with the availability of foreign exchange, government income would be cut back also. And though some money could be and was saved by such measures as official salary cuts and a slowdown in public works,[17] from the Colombian standpoint a far more attractive solution, to this problem and to others, was to borrow some more millions from the United States.

It was some time, naturally, before the full effect of the war was felt. Yet as early as September 2, 1939, Foreign Minister López de Mesa was already suggesting a standby credit of $50 million,

12. Secretary of State to Braden, July 15, 1939, and Braden to Secretary of State, July 18, 1939, FR (1939), V, 488-89; Laurence Duggan, memo, July 28, 1939, FR (1939), V, 498-500; MemHda (1940), pp. 139-40.
13. MemHda (1940), pp. 24-25; below, p. 83.
14. MemHda (1940), pp. 35-38.   15. Ibid., pp. 46-48.
16. The percentage derived from the customs was 42.3 in 1937, 38.4 in 1938, and 46.0 in 1939 (Contraloría General de la República, Anuario general de estadística [1940], p. 147).
17. MemHda (1940), pp. 197-200; Memoria de Obras Públicas (1940), pp. v-vi and passim.

whose mere availability—whether or not it was actually used-—
would sustain confidence in the peso.[18] The Colombian delegation
to the Panama Conference importuned Undersecretary of State
Sumner Welles along somewhat similar lines.[19] From the start,
moreover, the United States was generally sympathetic; but Braden
in Bogotá and his superiors in Washington saw to it that the
Colombians did not forget the connection between the assistance
they desired and the settlement of past accounts. At the same time
the State Department now decided to take a more forceful role
in the negotiations between Colombia and her private creditors.
Heretofore its officials in Washington and Bogotá had intermit-
tently reminded and encouraged and had even made some suggestions as to possible terms on a personal, unofficial basis. Henceforth it would work actively and persistently to promote a meeting of minds between the Colombian government and the FBPC.
If, for example, Colombia would agree to a settlement at 3 per
cent interest rising by stages to 4.25 per cent, the State Department's Laurence Duggan assured the Colombian Ambassador in
Washington that the Department would use its influence to seek
acceptance of the same terms by the bondholder representatives.[20]

Colombia never did agree to go that high, but it is probably
safe to say that in the stepped-up negotiations that followed, the
State Department sided more often with Colombia than with the
FBPC.[21] The first concrete result emerged in February, 1940, when
the Colombian government announced that it would pay interest
on the 1927 and 1928 loans for the current year at the rate of 3
per cent and would devote an additional $400 thousand during
the year to the open-market purchase of bonds for retirement.[22]
Because of the bonds' depressed market price, the latter sum
ultimately permitted Colombia to acquire bonds with a face value
of about $1.8 million,[23] and the *New York Times* reported that
American bond specialists considered this method somewhat un-
fair;[24] but the FBPC did expressly approve the arrangements, even
if with no great enthusiasm.[25]

18. Braden to Secretary of State, Sept. 2, 1939, *FR* (1939), V, 501.
19. Welles to Secretary of State, Sept. 26, 1939, *FR* (1939), V, 504-5.
20. Duggan, memo, Sept. 19, 1939, *FR* (1939), V, 502-4.
21. Braden, it is worth noting, was always somewhat critical of the FBPC;
see, e.g., his letter to President Roosevelt, March 27, 1939, DS 711.21/933.
22. *N.Y.T.*, Feb. 13, 1940, 35:4.
23. *MemHda* (1940), p. 146.
24. *N.Y.T.*, Feb. 18, 1940, 1:2.
25. Braden to Secretary of State, Feb. 23, 1940, *FR* (1940), V, 697.

In any event, the February, 1940, temporary agreement was the first real breakthrough in United States-Colombian financial negotiations, and it obviously facilitated the granting of a $10 million Export-Import Bank loan to Colombia.[26] The loan was formally announced early in May and was made, not directly to the Colombian government, but to the semi-official Banco de la República. The result was the same because the bank immediately loaned the government the equivalent of $10 million in Colombian pesos—17.5 million, at the existing exchange rate. This money was earmarked for a broad range of projects designed to strengthen the Colombian economy in the war emergency and after, all along the lines of Lleras's proposals a year before to Ambassador Braden. To be exact, the loan amount (in pesos) was appropriated as shown in the table.[27]

Additional capital for the Caja de Crédito Agrario Industrial y Minero	7,000,000
Creation of an Instituto de Fomento Industrial	2,000,000
Highway construction	3,000,000
Railway construction and related port works (completion of Buenaventura-Medellín railroad; Nariño railroad; Tumaco port works)	2,000,000
Payment of part of the debt owed by the nation to the Consejo Administrativo de los Ferrocarriles Nacionales and acquisition of equipment for public works (including improvement of river navigation)	3,000,000
Establishment of a revolving fund for agricultural development in the Ministerio de la Economía Nacional	500,000

Since new requirements for foreign exchange arising out of this program would materialize only gradually, the Banco de la República could meanwhile use the greater part of the dollar proceeds of the loan to help liquidate a backlog of exchange arrears estimated in the neighborhood of $8 million.[28] Last but not least, the loan was sure to redound to the political benefit of the Santos administration, and this was another objective that the United States was perfectly willing to assist.

Meanwhile talks continued concerning a permanent settlement of the older debts. Some of the immediate pressure for a full adjustment may have been relieved by the granting of the Export-Import Bank loan, but Colombians still expected to come back for more United States credits later on, and there were naturally other

26. *N.Y.T.*, May 10, 1940, 41:5.
27. *MemHda* (1940), pp. 150-53.
28. Braden to Welles (memo), April 19, 1940, *FR* (1940), V, 699.

valid reasons to keep searching for an agreement. There was even a special reason for haste, because on July 20, 1940, the extraordinary economic powers voted to the Colombian Executive by Congress the previous December to deal with problems of the war emergency were due to expire. Santos and Lleras understandably wished to effect a settlement under these broad powers rather than go to Congress for the approval of specific terms, as otherwise they would have to do.

By now it was clear that Colombia would not accept more than a straight 3 per cent interest in any permanent settlement, and United States government representatives appear to have accepted this quite calmly, even though they had frequently expressed support either for a higher figure or for a gradually increasing rate. What was to become the definitive formula was advanced by Secretary of Commerce Jesse Jones at a meeting held in Washington on July 6, 1940, a meeting that was also attended by other United States officials, Colombian Ambassador Gabriel Turbay, and a representative of the FBPC. It entailed consolidation of the outstanding principal of the 1927 and 1928 issues, plus one-half of the arrears of interest, in a new debt bearing 3 per cent; Colombia was also to make provision for regular amortization, beginning on a very modest scale but later increasing.[29] The Colombian government gave approval to these terms but insisted on adding the provision that service might be temporarily suspended again, if the condition of Colombian finances made such a step absolutely necessary.[30] The FBPC, on its part, refused to approve the terms in question, feeling that it had been let down by the State Department in the matter of interest[31] and objecting vigorously to the conditional suspension feature. White insisted that rather than accept the latter he would prefer a mere renewal of the 1940 short-term agreement.[32] But as Duggan, for one, later pointed out, the suspension provision merely expressed overtly what was a sovereign prerogative of any government; if anything, he observed, Colombia was "perhaps . . . a little more honest in giving notice."[33]

Even without the concurrence of the FBPC, President Santos on July 17 issued a decree under his soon-to-expire emergency powers

29. Welles, memo, July 6, 1940, *FR* (1940), V, 706.
30. Colombian Embassy to Department of State, July 1 and 10, 1940, *FR* (1940), V, 705, 707.
31. See, e.g., Bonsal to Welles, Dec. 27, 1940, *FR* (1940), V, 718.
32. Duggan, memo, July 15, 1940, *FR* (1940), V, 708.
33. Duggan to Welles (memo), Dec. 13, 1940, *FR* (1940), V, 714.

setting forth certain "bases that the Government shall adopt for the service of the national external loans of 1927 and 1928."[34] These "bases" followed the Jones formula, with the addition of the suspension provision, and were naturally displeasing to bondholder spokesmen; but once the July 20 deadline had passed, Colombian officials insisted that they could not legally revise the terms on their own authority, and Sumner Welles informed White that the State Department saw no reason to question the Colombian interpretation.[35] Thus the specific settlement terms which at long last were formally announced in Washington on December 30 essentially confirmed what was already decided. They called for the exchange of outstanding 6 per cent bonds for new 3 per cent obligations of 25 to 30 years maturity, and capitalization on the same terms of one-half the unpaid interest. The value of the new issue was to be $50 million: i.e., approximately $43.7 million of the original principal that was still outstanding after the open-market purchases Colombia had made in the course of 1940, plus $6.3 million in interest arrears.[36] The suspension provision was not mentioned in the announcement—but it remained an understood condition of the settlement, by virtue of the July 17 decree.

A joint statement released to the press by the State and Treasury Departments and the Federal Loan Agency described the Colombian terms as "a fair effort on [Colombia's] part to adjust its obligations."[37] The FBPC, on the other hand, continued to sulk, assailing the terms as "entirely out of line with what Colombia can do" and discriminatory "against the bondholders in providing only 50 per cent interest while serving internal bonds and short-term credits in full." The FBPC statement called attention to the discrepancy between the 3 per cent interest Colombia was offering to private investors (with the United States' official blessing) and the 4 per cent which the Export-Import Bank was charging on its own recent loan to Colombia.[38] In a similar vein, a financial commentator in the New York *Herald-Tribune* accused the United

34. Ministerio de Hacienda y Crédito Público, *Decretos de carácter extraordinario expedidos por el Ejecutivo en desarrollo de las autorizaciones conferidas al Presidente de la República por la Ley 54 de 1939* (Bogotá, 1940), pp. 12-13.

35. Welles to Francis White, Dec. 20, 1940, *FR* (1940), V, 716.

36. *N.Y.T.*, Dec. 31, 1940, 26:1; *MemHda* (1941), pp. 30-31. Actually, the refunding operation did not call for quite $50 million; there was a difference of $127.50 in Colombia's favor.

37. *N.Y.T.*, Dec. 31, 1940, 26:1.

38. *N.Y.T.*, Jan. 1, 1941, 35:4.

States government of "aiding and abetting Colombia in bilking American citizens";[39] and the Council flatly refused to advise individual holders of Colombian securities to accept the terms.

Nevertheless, Colombia now proceeded to complete the required formalities of the transaction. One was to obtain the approval of the Colombian Junta Nacional de Empréstitos, a chiefly advisory body made up of Congressmen from both major parties. It gave its approval without dissent,[40] even though the Conservative members—one of whom was Senator Luis Ignacio Andrade, manager of *El Siglo*—later stipulated that they approved only the actual terms of the arrangement, not the device of offering those terms under the authority of extraordinary powers which had in fact expired by the time the offer was announced.[41] The Conservative opposition had often raised a great hue and cry over smaller technicalities than this, but in the present case no serious issue was made of the alleged breach of legality. (A more fundamental Conservative criticism was simply that the loan settlement should have been made sooner than it was, since one of the countless sins attributed to the Liberal regime had been precisely its destruction of Colombia's favorable credit standing abroad.[42]) The sourest Colombian reaction, as a matter of fact, is probably that which came from the López wing of the Liberal Party itself. One *lopista* spokesman suggested in *El Liberal* that the Santos administration had been taken in by a clever United States diplomatic maneuver aiming to make new financial assistance appear dependent on the settlement of old debts—whereas, in practice, the United States was determined to force credits on Latin American countries no matter what, so that their purchasing could take the place of European markets lost since the outbreak of war. But the López Liberals did not make a special issue of the loan settlement either; in their view, it was just one of various things that Colombia had recently done for the United States without receiving adequate compen-

39. New York *Herald-Tribune*, Jan. 1, 1941, 31:4.
40. *T.*, Feb. 23, 1941; *N.Y.T.*, Feb. 24, 1941, 28:3.
41. *S.*, May 11, 1941.
42. This last criticism was quite clearly expressed in an editorial of *La Patria* (Manizales), Jan. 9, 1941. But from the Conservative standpoint the blame for delay had to be shared by both the Liberals and the United States. The latter was taken to task by *El Siglo*, for example, for its obstinate resistance (*"conducta rebelde"*) to the necessary scaling down of interest charges (*S.*, May 31, 1940).

sation in the form of Export-Import Bank credits or otherwise.[43]

The very last details to be taken care of were the signing of contracts with financial agents in the United States to handle the conversion of the old issues into the new one and the payment of future interest and amortization, and the making of a formal offer of conversion directly to the bondholders. All this was finally accomplished in May and June, 1940, and despite the attitude of the FBPC the rate of response from individual investors was quite satisfactory. In just the first eight months 80 per cent of the United States bondholders had indicated their acceptance.[44]

Even before the actual completion of these arrangements, the State Department was calling on its Embassy in Bogotá to see what might be done on behalf of other groups of creditors, while the Colombian government was broaching the subject of still another Export-Import Bank loan.[45] Once again discussion proceeded on both topics simultaneously; but the new loan proved easier to arrange. The original Colombian request was for $10 million, to be used for both military and economic requirements.[46] The question of military assistance was soon separated from that of economic aid, to be handled instead through lend-lease channels,[47] but as negotiations progressed the Colombian want-list grew longer, until $13 million was being requested for economic aid alone. That sum was quite apart from a possible currency-stabilization loan which the Colombians now mentioned again, even though Braden was unconvinced of the need. Neither did he approve of all the other Colombian requests. He did not question the desirability of credits for essential public works, some of which were being curtailed because of the drop in Colombian customs revenues, and for irrigation and drainage projects in the banana zone, whose basic crop was currently hard hit by an epidemic of sigatoka disease. But he was skeptical about some other proposed development projects and noted that the Instituto de Fomento Industrial set up largely with funds from the previous year's loan had so far

43. See article by Jorge Zalamea in *L.*, March 9, 1941, and López's own charges that United States cooperation had been inadequate in *L.*, Jan. 25 and April 15, 1941.

44. *MemHda* (1941), pp. 39-62; Livesey, memo, March 6, 1942, *FR* (1942), VI, 217; *N.Y.T.*, June 5, 1941, 33:4 and June 7, 1941, 25:2.

45. Braden to Secretary of State, Feb. 3, 1941, and Welles to Braden, March 27, 1941, *FR* (1941), VII, 55-56.

46. Braden, memo, April 16, 1941, *FR* (1941), VII, 57.

47. Above, pp. 55-57.

invested only one-fifth of its capital in new undertakings (none of which, he claimed, were as yet known to be in operation). Finally, there was no doubt that Santos was eager to borrow more money in part simply to refute the insinuations of Alfonso López that he had not been sufficiently forceful in extracting aid from the United States.[48]

Nevertheless, in the last analysis, neither Braden in Bogotá nor his superiors in Washington were much inclined to quibble. Santos was a proven friend; a few million dollars would never be missed. Not only this, but the Bogotá press, apparently with official encouragement, was holding out the expectation that Colombia would get essentially what she wanted, thus creating a situation in which it would have been awkward to do much less.[49] So, by a contract signed July 23, 1941, Colombia was granted $12 million from the Export-Import Bank, again at 4 per cent interest.[50] Or, as one writer put it this· time in *El Siglo*, "the future of the nation has been burdened again and more heavily."[51] But the Conservatives did not really seem to mind very much, and *lopistas* were happy to note that the administration had apparently taken to heart their own pronouncements on the previous insufficiency of United States aid. *El Liberal* even suggested that the shift in policy was due to Lleras Restrepo's departure from the ministry the previous March.[52]

The new loan was made directly to the Colombian government rather than to the Banco de la República. The entire amount was not immediately paid over to Colombia, nor was it all earmarked in advance for specific objectives; even as late as 1943 there was still a modest balance awaiting appropriation. But somewhat over half was in fact destined for highway construction and improvements. The next largest amount went for irrigation and drainage works, and something was used after all, with United States approval, for defense expenditures—for air bases, military buildings, and equipment. General agricultural development, naviga-

48. Emilio G. Collado, memo, May 2, 1941, Duggan, memo, May 22, 1941, and Braden to Secretary of State, May 29, 1941, *FR* (1941), VII, 61-63, 66-68.

49. Collado, memo, May 2, 1941, and Keith to Secretary of State, May 10, 1941, *FR* (1941), VII, 61-65.

50. Welles to Braden, July 25, 1941, *FR* (1941), VII, 72. The loan negotiations were not actually complete until the approval of the terms by the Colombian Congress in October (*N.Y.T.*, Oct. 5, 1941, 36:5).

51. S., June 15, 1941.

52. L., June 14, 1941.

tion and port works, and construction of other government build-ings all received lesser shares.[53]

Once the Export-Import Bank loan of 1941 was granted, the efforts of the Santos administration to obtain further credits from the United States were mainly concerned with military require-ments; the end result was the lend-lease agreement of March, 1942.[54] At the same time, however, the Colombian government continued to work for a settlement of its other outstanding dollar obligations, and before Santos left office, agreement had been reached on both Olaya's banking-group loan and the obligations of the Banco Agrícola Hipotecario. In the former case, Colombia had been gradually whittling away at the principal, which during 1939, for example, was reduced by more than a quarter of a million dollars. Gradually, too, the area of disagreement on terms for a permanent settlement was being narrowed by discussions between the Colombian government and the bankers, with occa-sional discreet prodding from the State Department but with little sense of real urgency on either side. The main issue at stake was the length of time to be allowed for complete liquidation, since Colombia wanted a fifteen-year period, and some but not all of the banking firms insisted on ten. In the end, what was ostensibly a compromise was adopted. By an agreement of May, 1942, provision was made for regular quarterly payments over a ten-year period, but with the last payment, due December 31, 1952, amounting to $5,578,896. Colombia was not expected to satisfy that amount in a lump sum; it would have to be renegotiated when the time came, so that the date of final liquidation was still left undeter-mined.[55]

Really serious discussions concerning the mortgage-bank debts began only in September, 1941, when the Banco Agrícola Hipo-tecario proposed that service be resumed on the guaranteed issues at 2.5 per cent interest, with back interest to be forgiven. Some-what comparable treatment was offered in the case of the non-guaranteed issues for which it had assumed responsibility, though details were not spelled out. The State Department, however, in-

53. Secretary of State to Embassy in Bogotá, Feb. 9, 1942, DS 821.24/195; MemHda (1943), p. 46.

54. Below, pp. 108-9.

55. Braden to Secretary of State, Nov. 10, 1941, FR (1941), VII, 77-78; Braden to Secretary of State, Feb. 13, 1942, and Collado, memos, Feb. 28 and March 6, 1942, FR (1942), VI, 210-12; MemHda (1940), p. 155; MemHda (1941), p. 281; MemHda (1943), p. 45.

formed the special negotiator sent to Washington by the bank that the terms appeared too low—that the creditors should not obtain less than the terms recently offered national bondholders. The bank then came up with a revised proposal which was endorsed in principle by State Department officials, and after further detailed negotiations was embodied in a formal offer to the bondholders in June, 1942. It called for the holders of guaranteed bonds to receive new 3 per cent Colombian national bonds at the rate of $1,100 for each $1,000 of principal, the additional $100 representing partial compensation for interest arrears. Nonguaranteed bonds were to be exchanged at the rate of $750 in new bonds for each $1,000 of the old. These final terms were expressly approved in advance by the Department of State, and they affected a total of slightly more than $10 million in bonds outstanding in the hands of United States investors.[56]

Thus by the time Santos left office only the holders of municipal and departmental bonds were still waiting for some form of settlement, although the creditors of the Department of Cundinamarca did at least obtain a judicial warrant of attachment in New York against the paltry sum of $42,725 owed to the Department by its United States fiscal agents.[57] In any event, the Santos administration had redeemed its pledge to do something about the state of Colombian foreign credit. It had worked out a series of refunding operations on terms that were generally closer to the original Colombian official position than to that of the foreign creditors. And in so doing, the Santos administration had kept domestic political criticism to a minimum, while it successfully met one of the key conditions for receiving new loans from the United States government. These new loans, moreover, set a pattern which has continued to the present and which shows no sign of ending.

56. James H. Wright, memo, Oct. 31, 1941, *FR* (1941), VII, 75-77; Livesey, memos, Jan. 15 and 27, 1942, and Department of State to Colombian Embassy, March 19, 1942, *FR* (1942), VI, 205-9, 218-19; *Commercial and Financial Chronicle*, June 25, 1942, p. 2387.
57. *N.Y.T.*, March 12, 1941, 32:2.

Coffee, Bananas, Oil

LOAN NEGOTIATIONS were only one aspect of Colombian-United States economic relations during the Santos administration, and despite the amount of official attention they received they were not necessarily the most important. Indeed, the key fact of economic relations continued to be the overwhelming leadership enjoyed by the United States as a source of Colombian imports and as a market for Colombian exports. A similar position of leadership existed in the field of direct private investments. Neither trade nor direct investments, however, presented a static picture. In either case the changing international situation had far-reaching repercussions, and in the field of investments there were also continuing problems of domestic economic policy that directly affected foreign-owned enterprises.

I

In 1938, the last full prewar year, coffee had provided 54.4 per cent of the value of Colombian export trade, and even this figure does not do full justice to the pervasive importance of the international coffee market for Colombia. The second- and third-ranking exports—crude petroleum and gold, which in 1938 contributed

22.8 per cent and 11.5 per cent respectively[1]—employed a relatively minor percentage of the national labor force. Coffee was by contrast a labor-intensive crop, grown in virtually every major section of the republic on large estates and small peasant properties alike. Coffee was of particular significance, furthermore, in United States-Colombian relations, for despite the recent growth of German purchases paid for in compensation marks, the United States retained first place as a buyer of Colombian coffee by a substantial margin. The United States in 1938 took 80 per cent of Colombian coffee exports and Germany took 16 per cent, as against 84 per cent and 7 per cent just four years earlier.[2]

The pattern of the Colombian coffee trade, with its heavy dependence on the United States market, gave a degree of built-in protection against drastic loss of export volume following the outbreak of World War II. It did not, however, give equal protection against a decline in export value, which was dependent on conditions in the world coffee trade as a whole; and the virtual closing of the German market at the beginning of the European war, followed by the loss of still other continental markets as the war progressed, had notably adverse effects on coffee prices. From September 11, 1939, to September 4, 1940, the New York price of the basic Colombian coffee type (Manizales) went from 12.75 cents per pound to 7.25 cents—nearly the lowest on record.[3] This decline not only reduced the income of the coffee industry but threatened a fiscal crisis for the Colombian government itself. The relationship between coffee prices and sales and government revenue was inevitably complex, but the source of greatest immediate concern was the fact that any major loss of foreign-exchange earnings—such as the present coffee situation inevitably entailed—would diminish Colombia's capacity to import. This in turn threatened the yield of the customs, the most important single source of tax revenue.

Even before the full impact of the declining coffee price was felt, the Santos administration began adopting countermeasures. Exchange-control regulations were tightened, starting in Decem-

---

1. W. H. Delaplane, "The War and an Agricultural Economy: The Case of Colombia," *The Southern Economic Journal,* IX (July, 1942), 34.

2. Contraloría General de la República, *Anuario de comercio exterior* (1938), pp. 78-79. Percentages given in the text are based on value. (Much of the coffee exported to Germany was actually resold in other countries of Europe.)

3. Delaplane, "The War and an Agricultural Economy," p. 36.

ber, 1939, and special restrictions were placed on certain types of imports. The government moved to increase the production and export of gold; as mentioned in the preceding chapter, it speeded up financial negotiations with the United States in order to obtain new foreign credits; and in May, 1940, it established a bounty of two pesos a bag on coffee exports.[4] All these expedients appear to have been of some help. But except for the export bounty they did not directly assist the coffee industry, nor was there any assurance that their combined effect would solve the foreign-exchange problem. Hence Colombia, in concert with other Latin America producers, turned to the further expedient of cooperative action to support the price of coffee.

The idea of an inter-American agreement to limit coffee production and exports and thereby maintain the price at an acceptable level was far from new, but it had not generally enjoyed much favor in Colombia. Confident that the superior quality of their own grades of coffee would guarantee the sale of all they produced—and at a price comfortably above that of the Brazilian product—Colombians had normally preferred to go their own way in the world coffee market. In 1936, to be sure, with strong support from the López administration, the quasi-official Federación Nacional de Cafeteros did enter into an agreement with Brazil for joint restriction of exports. But the federation could not adequately finance its share of the program, which is one reason—though certainly not the only one—why the agreement quickly broke down.[5] The new situation brought on by World War II then created sentiment in Colombia for another try at international regulation, and when the Third Pan American Coffee Conference convened at New York in June, 1940, to devise a plan of joint action, Colombia was an active collaborator.

The United States, fearing especially the political consequences of economic distress, was also prepared to collaborate, an even more important augury of success. The main conditions imposed by the State Department, as expressed in a message from Secretary Cordell Hull to the president of the Coffee Conference, were that the United States should be officially represented in the formulation and administration of the program and that the in-

---

4. *Ibid.*, pp. 38-40.
5. Mariano Ospina Pérez, "La política cafetera colombiana," *Revista Colombiana*, V (May 1, 1935), 69-76; *MemHda* (1941), p. 15; *MemHda* (1942), pp. 75-76.

terests of consumers as well as producers must be taken into account.[6] However, the Latin Americans would apparently have preferred, as at least a first step, not to impose limitations on themselves but simply to have non-American coffee excluded from the United States market. Only when it became clear that the United States could not accept such a solution did the Conference begin "serious discussion" of a general quota system,[7] and even then the actual fixing of quotas was an extremely complicated and difficult matter. Indeed the Conference managed only to draw up a tentative plan which was left to be perfected through further negotiations among the Pan American Coffee Bureau, the Inter-American Financial and Economic Advisory Committee in Washington (which was headed by Sumner Welles), and the interested governments themselves, including that of the United States.

Colombia, though she came to accept the quota system in principle, created probably more than her share of difficulties. The Colombian delegation at New York raised objections to the idea of coffee import quotas to be enforced by the United States, preferring to rely on export quotas at the Latin American end, even though United States participation in the enforcement process was the best guarantee of effectiveness. In later negotiations over the size of specific national quotas, the Colombian government insisted on haggling over quite insignificant quantities—virtually admitting, furthermore, that its reasons were political, not economic. Unfortunately, the quota discussions reached their climax during September and October, 1940, precisely when the Santos administration was facing major problems in Congress over the Havana agreements, the proposed defense loan, and so forth; and it was frankly afraid that a difference of a few thousand bags in a quota slated to exceed three million would bring dangerous political repercussions on the home front. Nevertheless, Colombia in the end had little choice but to yield. An Inter-American Coffee Agreement was formally signed both by Latin American exporting nations and by the United States on November 28, 1940, assigning Colombia a quota in the United States market of 3,150,000 bags out of a total of 15,545,000 for all coffee exporters. This was 50,000 less than Colombia had sought, though not quite so far from her last bargaining position. The final formula for the dis-

6. Hull to Manuel Mejía, June 24, 1940, *FR* (1940), V, 381-82.
7. Paul C. Daniels, memo, July 3, 1940, *FR* (1940), V, 383.

tribution of quotas was in considerable part the work of the United States, which also agreed to share in the work of enforcing them.[8]

Despite its previous objections, the Colombian government hailed the Coffee Agreement after it materialized as a major economic achievement. It would be hard to find a more "brilliant" operation, declared the 1941 *Memoria* of the Ministry of Finance,[9] which gave due credit to the United States for helping to bring it about. The basis for this satisfaction was the fact that the downward trend of coffee prices had been successfully reversed in the latter part of 1940. The recovery began even before the Agreement was signed, but at least partly in anticipation of its effect; and by mid-1941 the price of Manizales had more than doubled, to a level of 16 to 17 cents per pound.[10] This happy ending was not, of course, due solely to the quota pact, because coffee consumption was rising steadily in the United States under the influence of defense employment and other factors. Thus by May, 1941, it was already possible to assign the exporting nations, including Colombia, a round of increases in their quotas, and other increases kept coming at regular intervals without pushing the price of coffee downward again; indeed one of the reasons for the larger quotas was to keep the price from rising too sharply.[11]

Unofficial opinion in Colombia was less ecstatic about the quota system. Many Conservatives, especially, felt that even if the Coffee Agreement had been beneficial in the short run, Colombia would be better off in the end if she continued to rely on quality production rather than market manipulation.[12] The López faction of Liberals offered no such criticism of the quota principle but minimized the concrete benefit derived from the 1940 agreement and insisted that it was at least as valuable to the United States as to Colombia—for example, that increased coffee earnings went right

8. On these negotiations, see the collected memos, dispatches, etc., in *FR* (1940), V, 382-405; *MemHda* (1940), pp. 27-31; *MemHda* (1941), pp. 117-18; World Peace Foundation, *Documents on American Foreign Relations, July 1940-June 1941* (Boston, 1941), pp. 97-106 (for the text of the agreement); Paul C. Daniels, "The Inter-American Coffee Agreement," *Law and Contemporary Problems*, VIII (Autumn, 1941), 708-20.

9. *MemHda* (1941), p. 23.

10. Delaplane, "The War and an Agricultural Economy," p. 36. The price then roughly stabilized and was still at the same level a year later (*MemHda* [1942], p. 94).

11. *MemHda* (1941), p. 19; *MemHda* (1942), pp. 91-92; Daniels, "The Inter-American Coffee Agreement," p. 718.

12. See, e.g., *La Patria* (Manizales), March 4, 1941.

back in payment for American exports.[13] There was also some grumbling over the structure of official controls and special taxes that the government imposed, in collaboration with the Federación Nacional de Cafeteros, to take coffee stocks in excess of the export quota off the market and hold them in storage. But the federation itself, whose top echelons included a strong representation of Conservatives, stood by the government and the agreement.[14] Discontent was also lessened by the mere fact that the coffee industry, for whatever reasons, was thriving. During the entire year 1940 the volume of coffee exports had risen while the value actually fell, but in 1941 it was the other way around, and in 1942 both rose sharply together (see the table[15]). In this fashion coffee continued playing the major role in Colombian export trade, and the coffee recovery—combined with intensification of gold production and exports—far more than offset the total collapse that soon overtook the banana trade.[16]

COLOMBIAN COFFEE EXPORTS

Year	Bags	Pesos
1938	4,228,801	88,775,329
1939	3,702,163	87,124,693
1940	4,443,199	74,023,042
1941	2,911,518	83,293,779
1942	4,309,479	144,750,690

II

Banana exports from Colombia in 1938 amounted to 8,883,871 pesos, or 5 per cent of total exports. The United States took only 49 per cent of this amount, as against 80 per cent for coffee,[17] but the industry was dominated by the United Fruit Company of Boston, and the never-ending troubles of United Fruit caused bananas to loom disproportionately large in United States-Colombian relations. Though the company produced only about one-fifth of all Colombian banana exports on its own lands,[18] it purchased virtually all the rest of the exportable crop from independent growers for shipment on its own account to Europe or North

13. *L.*, March 9, 1941.
14. Delaplane, "The War and an Agricultural Economy," p. 41; *MemHda* (1941), p. 22. The federation had, of course, played an important part in negotiating the Coffee Agreement for Colombia.
15. Based on *Anuario de comercio exterior*, 1938-42.
16. See Appendix.
17. *Anuario de comercio exterior* (1938), pp. 2, 3, 78-79, 206.
18. Greene to Secretary of State, Oct. 6, 1938, DS 821.6156/262.

America. It thus exercised, in effect, a marketing if not a producing monopoly, and this had long been a source of irritation in Colombia. It would lie outside the scope of this study to examine how much truth (if any) there may have been in charges that United Fruit consistently rigged prices and other conditions of the banana business in its own favor, yet the mere existence of such charges inevitably affected not just the company's public image but Colombian official attitudes and regulatory decisions concerning it.[19]

Certainly no other foreign-owned enterprise had felt the displeasure of the López administration to the same extent as had United Fruit. Believing that the company had used its purchasing contracts to reduce independent growers to an unhealthy state of servitude, the López regime sponsored Law 1 of 1937 which among other things limited the standard contracts to a maximum duration of two years. It also put through what was ostensibly a much more sweeping measure, enacted later the same year, which provided for an ill-defined government "intervention" in the banana industry and authorized the use of expropriation if necessary to achieve its objectives.[20] The practical effects of both measures had been slight,[21] but they were not the only evidence of official hostility. Indeed, the company was subjected to what it considered a campaign of pure harassment, which led twice to the arrest of its resident manager (on charges that were ultimately dismissed).[22] Whether the treatment it received was deserved or not, it was natural enough for United Fruit to conceive doubts as to its future in Colombia; and one result was an obvious hesitation to expand its Colombian operations further or even to main-

19. The record of the United Fruit Company is examined fully but not exhaustively—and most of the complaints usually made against it disproved to the authors' satisfaction—in Stacy May and Galo Plaza, *The United Fruit Company in Latin America* (Washington, 1958). The information specifically relating to United Fruit operations in Colombia (pp. 12, 175-80, and *passim*) is unfortunately rather limited. See also J. Fred Rippy, *The Capitalists and Colombia* (New York, 1931), pp. 180-88.

20. *Leyes* (Jan.-June, 1937), p. 4; *Leyes* (July-Dec., 1937), pp. 95-96.

21. With respect to the contract feature of Law 1, there had been a rush to make longer contracts just before the law was enacted, which lessened its immediate impact since it was not retroactively applied (Dawson to Secretary of State, Aug. 27, 1937, DS 821.6156/230). Ambassador Braden, however, came to the conclusion that the length of contracts was greatly overrated in importance by both the company and its critics and that it would make little difference in practice if the company bought bananas with no contracts at all (Braden to Secretary of State, May 8, 1939, DS 821.6156/264).

22. Greene to Secretary of State, Jan. 21, 1938, DS 821.6156/253; *La Defensa Social* (Bogotá), Nov. 29, 1939.

tain their current level. What made the situation particularly disturbing for the company—and for Colombia—was the fact that since late in 1937 there had been clear indications of the spread of sigatoka disease in Colombian banana plantations.[23] The disease could be controlled, but only by complex and costly measures which United Fruit did not wish to undertake unless it had greater assurance of stability for its position in Colombia.

The chances for a successful rapprochement were seemingly improved in 1938 both by the arrival of a new manager for United Fruit and by the change in administration at Bogotá. Soon after taking office, President Santos had a cordial talk with Reginald H. Hamer, the new head of the company's operations, in which he emphasized that there was no longer any need to fear hostile treatment. Santos's Minister of National Economy added further specific assurance that the government intended no expropriation of banana lands, with the possible exception of a few strips to be used for irrigation works or telephone right-of-way or something equally innocuous. However, United Fruit was still hesitant to undertake a massive anti-sigatoka campaign. Hamer informed the United States Legation that the company would cooperate with any measures the Colombian government saw fit to take but that it would make no special effort on its own; and if the industry should ultimately be ruined, he added, United Fruit was prepared to leave Colombia without regrets.[24]

The persistence of public and political suspicion of United Fruit was demonstrated early in the Santos administration by the formal accusation, lodged by the Chamber of Representatives, against a former Minister of Education, Pedro María Carreño, for allegedly having exerted improper influence on the fruit company's behalf in adjusting terms for the rental of one of its ships as a troop carrier during the Leticia crisis between Colombia and Peru. The aggravating circumstance in this incident, which was by now rather ancient, was that Carreño had been receiving payments as a legal adviser to United Fruit despite his position in the Colombian cabinet.[25] It thus served as handy confirmation of the stock charge that the fruit company had been suborning Colombian politicians

23. Dawson to Secretary of State, Nov. 9, 1937, DS 821.6156/244.
24. Greene to Secretary of State, Oct. 6, 1938, DS 821.6156/262.
25. *S.,* March 23, 1938; *T.,* March 31, 1938, and *passim.* Carreño insisted that the payments in question (which were quite small) were intended for his son, who was handling legal work for United Fruit while he was in the cabinet; but they were declared on his, not his son's, income tax.

to serve its nefarious ends, and the fact that Carreño was a Conservative member of Olaya Herrera's coalition regime when the incident occurred gave added zest to the attacks of Colombian Liberals, principally of the López faction.

The move for a retroactive impeachment of Carreño had actually begun toward the end of the López administration; it merely came to a head after Santos took office. The Senate eventually voted, in November, 1938, not to admit the accusation presented by the lower house, but its decision specified that Carreño's conduct—and thus, by extension, that of the fruit company—was deserving of censure.[26] Nor did the Senate's decision immediately end agitation on the matter, which dragged on for a while longer.[27] However, Carreño at least had the support of fellow Conservatives, and not just Conservative lawyers for foreign companies, since he was defended with vigor by Laureano Gómez's *El Siglo*.[28] Gómez and his immediate associates were chiefly concerned only with clearing the name of Carreño personally, but the latter was not, strictly speaking, a fellow *laureanista*, and they were not always tolerant of Conservatives who had served both foreign corporations and Olaya. It just happened that the Gómez brand of anti-Americanism generally spared that symbol of all Yankee economic exploitation, the United Fruit Company. The feud between López and United Fruit was obviously one major reason for this phenomenon; thereafter, Conservative leaders including Gómez were likely to trace anything that went wrong in the banana zone back to the "socialistic" antagonism of López toward private enterprise, with United Fruit (like any López victim) enjoying an automatic presumption of innocence. But the fact that Conservatives tended to be "soft" on United Fruit did not solve its problems. It meant that Santos could hold out the hand of friendship without fear of Laureano Gómez, but he still had his own party to contend with.

He also had to contend with United Fruit, which was regrettably slow to forgive and forget. The company continued to nurse its resentment over López's banana legislation, which it expressed directly in memoranda to the government and indirectly by having its attorneys advise a group of Colombian growers who chose to challenge the constitutionality of the intervention law in the courts. Meanwhile, sigatoka continued to spread, and the government's

26. *T.*, Nov. 10, 1938.
27. See, e.g., *Tierra* (Bogotá), Nov. 18, 1938.
28. See especially *S.*, March 23 and 25, 1938.

measures against it were quite inadequate. United Fruit still offered cooperation to the official campaign—e.g., lending the services of an expert in tropical agriculture, Dr. Wilson Popenoe—but it scrupulously refrained from taking the initiative.[29]

This, then, was one of the more pressing problems that Spruille Braden had to deal with after he arrived in Bogotá early in 1939 as United States Ambassador. He talked to both Colombian and United Fruit officials in the hope of fostering some sort of understanding, and he did obtain from the company an agreement to do what was required to save one portion of the banana lands it owned itself. In mid-April, furthermore, the Santos administration came up with what seemed a promising proposal. It was that the government should enter into an express agreement with the company which would clarify certain features of the intervention law and thereby give the company the confidence it needed before launching an all-out attack on sigatoka. Braden greeted this proposal with enthusiasm, and company officials on the scene agreed to recommend it to their Boston headquarters. But neither side pressed for quick implementation of the idea.[30]

The intervention law was largely eliminated as a relevant issue when the Colombian Supreme Court, in September, 1939, did in fact declare major portions of it unconstitutional. This decision, together with Santos's generally friendly attitude, should have gone far to eliminate the company's reservations about making the investment needed to curb sigatoka. Unfortunately, September, 1939, also saw the outbreak of war in Europe, which was a serious complication since European markets had been absorbing the majority of Colombian banana exports. The company did seek to lessen the war's impact by diverting a larger share of Colombian bananas to the North American market, even at the expense of other Caribbean producers, but the international situation still clouded even further the outlook for the Colombian banana industry.[31] Nevertheless, negotiations continued between company and government. What gradually emerged was a plan whereby the government would enter into a special contract with United Fruit, authorizing the company to conduct anti-sigatoka measures throughout the banana zone, including independently owned

29. Braden to Secretary of State, May 8 and Oct. 30, 1939, DS 821.6156/264, 270.

30. Braden to Secretary of State, May 8, 1939, DS 821.6156/264.

31. Braden to Secretary of State, Sept. 21 and 29, 1939, DS 821.6156/267, 268.

lands; in the latter case, the company would be empowered to make purchase contracts for longer than two years and recoup its expenditures by deductions from the price of fruit. The scheme was certainly reasonable—but no such contract was actually signed until April, 1941.

Both sides shared responsibility for this delay, during which the disease continued to spread and both production and exports to decline. (See Appendix.) The company, on its part, sought assurances of stability in Colombian wage scales and the like, and it temporarily withdrew late in 1940 its acceptance even of the principle of the proposed contract when the war shipping shortage caused Great Britain to prohibit banana imports entirely. On repeated occasions, the need of Hamer and other company officials in Colombia to consult their home office in Boston on important decisions was a handicap to the negotiations. In general, the company just did not give the appearance of an eager negotiator, but while its attitude may have been in part a bargaining stratagem, as Colombians suspected, there can be little doubt of its sincere lack of enthusiasm concerning its position in Colombia.[32] Nor is there much reason to doubt that one reason why it was willing to cooperate as far as it did was the recognition, strongly fostered by the Embassy in Bogotá and the State Department in Washington, that such cooperation would be in the United States as well as the Colombian national interest.

Bureaucratic nitpicking on the Colombian side, the regular turnover in Ministers of National Economy, and the need to adopt enabling legislation—all over and above the ingrained and continuing Colombian suspicions of United Fruit—must also share the blame for delay.[33] But Colombian obstructionism had its full flowering only *after* the sigatoka-control contract was signed in April, 1941. The contract gave the company general direction of the program, subject to ultimate government approval; the right to enter into direct contractual arrangements with participating independent growers for periods even up to ten years; and the right

32. Braden to Secretary of State, July 17, Dec. 13 and 30, 1940, and Feb. 24, 1941, DS 821.6156/274, 279, 281, 283. The problem posed by the closing of the British market was not so much the loss of British sales by Colombia as the need to give back to Jamaica some of the Jamaican share of the North American market which had been diverted to Colombia at the beginning of the war.

33. United Fruit Company, memo to Herbert Feis, Oct. 21, 1941, DS 821.6156/299; Braden to Secretary of State, Oct. 22, 1940, DS 821.6156/278.

to import duty-free needed supplies for the program. It also instructed the company to draw up a map indicating precisely which areas of the banana zone were suitable for anti-sigatoka treatment, since it was recognized that many banana plantations were too marginal to warrant the expenditure on special facilities, labor, and supplies that the treatment required and would thus have to be converted to other uses.[34] However, producers who found that they were to be excluded from the program against their will were quick to protest, and they found a hearing in Bogotá. Thus in September, 1941, the Ministry of National Economy officially disapproved the company's map and at the same time canceled the contract itself, on the grounds that the one imposed "an arbitrary limit" on the cultivable zone and the other represented "a colonial statute for the banana industry." The Ministry did authorize any growers who were to have been covered by the program as previously planned to work things out privately with United Fruit, but even in this case it set conditions the company would not accept.[35]

Part of the explanation for this fiasco was the mere fact that between April and September there had been another change in Ministers. A more general factor was the increasing influence of the López wing of the Liberal Party upon and within the Santos administration,[36] as the time approached for new presidential elections in which the former president was destined to run again as the government candidate. There was strong protest, of course, from many of the independent growers, but the chief political criticism of the government's action came from Conservatives, who regarded this as one more disgraceful episode in the campaign of persecution originally launched by Alfonso López against the banana industry.[37]

Actually, the disaster was not quite complete. Even while negotiations for the April, 1941, contract were in progress, United Fruit had finally moved to expand its own efforts against the sigatoka disease. Above all, it had undertaken the steps needed to save its own properties, or at least those company plantations it considered worth saving.[38] Thus it was only the Colombian growers who faced

---

34. *MemEcNac* (1941), pp. 133-36.
35. Braden to Secretary of State, Aug. 5 and Sept. 19, 1941, DS 821.6156/ 294, 297; *L.*, Sept. 13 and 20, 1941.
36. Braden to Welles, Oct. 9, 1941, DS 821.00/1369.
37. See, e.g., *S.*, Sept. 18 and Nov. 17, 1941; *L.*, Sept. 20, 1941.
38. *MemEcNac* (1941), pp. 131-32.

ultimate ruin. In the short run, United Fruit tried to go back to business more or less as usual, and it kept on buying some fruit from independent producers even when market and shipping conditions made its sale highly problematical. It also reported increasing difficulties with government inspectors who certified as sound harvested fruit that the company sought to reject as unfit for export.[39] However, the United States' entry into World War II soon brought another change for the worse. The steady withdrawal of shipping from the banana trade to carry more essential cargo left United Fruit by the middle of 1942 with no regular outlet even for a reduced level of Colombian production. Under these circumstances, the company proposed to suspend commercial operations entirely—meanwhile maintaining its own plantations as a source of stock for an eventual rebirth of the Colombian banana industry.[40]

The Colombian government had really no choice but to accept the company's decision. It was accepted even by Alfonso López, the old antagonist of United Fruit, who had been re-elected in May for a new term to begin in August, 1942; apparently López's main wish was that the formal suspension of banana cuttings for export should occur before he was inaugurated, and for once the company was happy to go along with his desire. By this time, moreover, even if an agreement could have been reached to wage a general anti-sigatoka campaign of the type once contemplated, there was no possibility of obtaining the essential supplies from abroad.[41] For this as well as all the other reasons, independent producers would have to change either permanently or temporarily to other crops. Indeed, before the final suspension of production for export—even before the cancellation of the famous contract—the Colombian government was already inaugurating measures of technical and other assistance to help the inhabitants of the banana zone make the adjustment. These measures were not really enough, but the United Fruit Company loyally did its part, for example, by transferring to the government without charge lands that were suitable for a planned program of agrarian resettlement and diversification.[42]

39. *L.*, Dec. 20, 1941; Braden to Secretary of State, Dec. 18 and 29, 1941, DS 821.6156/302, 303.
40. Keith to Secretary of State, July 3, 1942, DS 821.6156/319.
41. *Ibid.*
42. *MemEcNac* (1941), p. 132; *MemEcNac* (1942), pp. 48-51; Braden to Secretary of State, Dec. 18, 1941, and Jan. 27, 1942, DS 821.6156/303, 308; *L.*, Jan. 24, 1942; Lane to Secretary of State, May 21, 1942, DS 821.6156/316.

Thanks precisely to the fact that the decline of the banana industry had begun long before the culmination of the shipping crisis, all parties were better prepared to cope with the final shutdown; but a heavy price was paid for that preparedness. All in all, bananas represented probably the one most glaring failure in the field of United States-Colombian relations in the period under consideration.

III

The petroleum industry, like the banana industry, offered an example of frequently strained relations between foreign private enterprise and the host country, but fortunately the end result was different. The private companies—which included Royal Dutch Shell as well as American firms—were on better terms with Alfonso López and his followers than was United Fruit, and for that very reason among others they did not enjoy the same favor with Conservatives. But at least they had no plant disease to worry about. And though petroleum was overtaken by gold as Colombia's second most important export during the Santos years, on the whole it held its own in absolute terms, until the full impact of the shipping crisis was felt in 1942. (See Appendix.)

As mentioned earlier,[43] the basic petroleum legislation as revised in 1936 under the auspices of the López administration was on the whole favorable to the companies. Even so, there were certain unfavorable features. One was the provision that no one person or entity could obtain rights of exploration and exploitation to more than 100,000 hectares except for (a) land on the eastern *llanos*, where the maximum was 200,000; (b) the huge De Mares and Barco concessions, held respectively under special contracts by the Tropical Oil Company, an Esso subsidiary, and the Colombian Petroleum Company, which was jointly owned by Texaco and Socony; and (c) generally speaking, land which had been in private hands since before October 28, 1873. If property was privately owned prior to that date, Colombian law vested petroleum rights in the surface owner; if it had come into private possession only later, or was still publicly owned, petroleum rights remained with the state. This legal quirk was naturally a godsend to lawyers, who earned good fees tracing the existence of private titles back before the cutoff date, but in practice most petroleum concessions involved government-owned subsoil deposits, and it

43. Above, p. 4.

was rather widely accepted that the hectarage limitations were unrealistically low. They were often evaded, with the tacit consent of the Colombian authorities, by establishing subsidiaries or third-party fronts through which a single company obtained control of additional concessions beyond its legal limit. But tacit consent was not a firm foundation to build on, and in fact Colombian regulatory policy on this point had not been wholly consistent.[44]

Another undesirable feature of Colombian petroleum legislation was the requirement that a company conduct actual drilling on a government concession before the end of the period assigned for initial exploration. The purpose of the provision was to compel the companies to make a real effort to find oil rather than just accumulate concessions; but it could mean a needless expense if all preliminary survey data had clearly indicated that an area was not promising for commercial exploitation.[45] In this case there was no obvious way of getting around the law. It was only possible to hope that the government would make a special exception, or change the law so that a worthless concession could be formally given up without fulfilling the requirement.

While short-run solutions to these and other regulatory problems facing the petroleum companies were dependent on the attitude of Colombian officials in enforcing (or not enforcing) the law, long-range solutions could be found only in new legislation. In either case, the treatment to be accorded the industry involved more than strictly technical considerations, since in Colombia as elsewhere oil was a subject that impinged upon deeply felt aspirations of national dignity and independence. There were, to be sure, few Colombians who wished to emulate the recent Mexican example of oil expropriation, which had been greeted with outspoken sympathy by many Liberals and with bitter condemnation in *El Siglo*, in whose eyes Lázaro Cárdenas was even worse than Alfonso López.[46] For one thing, there was not yet enough to expropriate, since only Tropical with its installations centered at Barrancabermeja was producing oil commercially in significant quantities as of 1938. On the other hand, Colombian Petroleum's

44. Braden to Secretary of State, April 25, 1939, and Feb. 20, 1940, DS 821.6363/1310, 1346. *Leyes de 1936* (2nd ed., Bogotá, 1950), pp. 389-99, contains the petroleum law of 1936.
45. *MemMinas* (1941), pp. 41-43; Braden to Secretary of State, Feb. 10, 1941, DS 821.6363/1374.
46. See, e.g., *El Diario Nacional* (Bogotá), March 22 and 24, 1938, and S., March 29, 1938.

Barco concession in the Department of Norte de Santander was on the verge of large-scale production, and exploratory work in other parts of Colombia gave hope of still more to come.[47] Colombians were thus confident that their country had a major potential as an oil producer, and they meant to keep a tight rein on the industry, to make sure that the nation received full benefit from its subsoil wealth. They also tended to assume that foreign oil companies needed Colombian oil even more than Colombia needed their services in developing it, which was not necessarily the case.

To complicate matters further for the oil companies, their public image left something to be desired. The worldwide folklore of anti-imperialism and economic nationalism, which invariably ascribed sinister motives to the international oil industry, had made an impression in Colombia too. Moreover, even though there had been no major confrontation recently in Colombia between the government and any of the oil companies, there had been such confrontations in the past, and they had left a legacy of suspicion. That suspicion was not wholly unfounded, for at least some of the current practices of the companies were rather questionable. The evasion of hectarage limitations was perhaps a case in point. Another was the violation of legal provisions that required the oil companies to maintain a minimum percentage of Colombian nationals among their employees. This was another case in which the law itself was not quite realistic, for as yet there were not enough properly qualified Colombians to go around. The government itself recognized that full compliance was impossible and alternated between frank toleration of illegal employment practices and the imposition of rather modest fines. However, in this matter there was an escape clause allowing the companies to apply for special authorization to exceed the legal ratio of foreign employees, and they simply had not taken the trouble to do so.[48]

In the view of Ambassador Braden such practices, though perhaps understandable, were evidence of an overly casual attitude toward the laws and institutions of the host country. In certain other cases he lost patience entirely with the companies, as when it was an American pilot employed by Colombian Petroleum's pipeline affiliate—not one of the SCADTA Germans—who openly vio-

47. Eduardo Ospina-Racines, *La economía del petróleo en Colombia* (2nd ed., Bogotá, 1947), pp. 50-57, 116-20, and *passim*.
48. Braden to Secretary of State, April 25, 1939, DS 821.6363/1310; May 4 and Dec. 12 and 15, 1939, DS 821.504/109, 112, 113; *MemMinas* (1941), p. 181.

lated the Colombian decree of September, 1939, requiring a military copilot on every flight of a commercially owned aircraft.[49] The Ambassador had been equally indignant to discover soon after his arrival that Texaco up to the very last year had been helping its American employees defraud Colombia of income-tax revenue by reporting their salaries for tax purposes as if paid in pesos when actually the amounts were in dollars. The latter procedure was discontinued in 1939, but the company's manager (on the recommendation of his Colombian attorneys) did not take Braden's advice to make a clean breast of the situation to the Colombian authorities.[50]

In the last analysis, most of the sins of the oil companies were somewhat petty, often consisting of improper short cuts toward an objective which had official Colombian sanction: to locate and develop petroleum resources. However, it was their imaginary as well as their real sins that served to nourish the undercurrent of popular distrust. After all, the average citizen could not be expected to take much interest in the technical details of the hectarage-limitation problem, but he could find a wide array of more sensational charges that were voiced especially on the far left and on the right of the political spectrum. One noteworthy example was the series of articles published in *El Siglo*, in August, 1940—interspersed among its denunciations of the Havana agreements—about atrocities perpetrated by Colombian Petroleum upon the Motilón Indians.[51] There was, as a matter of fact, an endemic state of hostilities between employees at the company's Barco concession and the primitive Motilón tribe that lived in the vicinity, and at different times casualties had certainly been inflicted on the latter.[52] The company had by no means handled the problem as well as it might have. On the other hand, there was apparently no basis at just this point for the charges made in the Conservative organ to the effect that Yankee concessionnaires were even bombing and machine-gunning the Indians from the air. Worse yet, the campaign was taken up by Miguel Angel Builes, the irascible and ultra-reactionary Bishop of Santa Rosa de Osos in Antioquia, who addressed a letter of protest to President Santos in which he asserted that the Yankees "tomorrow . . . will do

49. Braden to Secretary of State, Oct. 30, 1939, DS 821.6363/1328.
50. Braden to Secretary of State, Feb. 16 and 27, 1939, DS 821.6363/1305, 1306.
51. S., Aug. 11, 24, 26, and 31, 1940.
52. Braden to Secretary of State, June 26, 1939, DS 821.6363/1313.

in the [Presidential Palace], in the Ministries, and in our cities what they are now doing to the natives in the jungle." Few educated Colombians, one may assume, took the bishop's prediction very seriously, but Santos did feel compelled to publicly reprimand him, while flatly denying the truth of the latest charges.[53]

In addition to playing up the plight of the Motilones, *El Siglo* on this and numerous other occasions accused Colombian Petroleum of maintaining its Colombian employees in a state of indescribable misery. Their condition, it once revealed, was one of "concentration camps and treatment as slaves."[54] Here again there was considerable exaggeration, although it was true that life on the Motilón frontier offered few civilized amenities and that the relatively superior accommodations provided there for American engineers made a galling contrast. It was even true that not all the provisions of Colombian labor legislation were literally observed in the company's field camps, but Colombian Petroleum achieved a worse reputation than it actually deserved, thanks to instances of tactless and discourteous treatment of Colombian officials, including labor inspectors. Fortunately Tropical, the largest company of all—which seems to have shown consistently more finesse at public relations—enjoyed both a better press and greater sympathy in government bureaus.[55]

In any case, the Ambassador was firmly convinced that the oil companies had a valid role to play in Colombian development and that fundamentally there was no conflict between their best interest and that of Colombia. Thus even while scolding and warning the companies over their assorted shortcomings, he devoted a major effort to seeking changes in the adverse provisions of Colombian petroleum legislation. He was particularly interested in modifying the hectarage limitations, as he considered the various methods of evasion both unethical and ultimately dangerous. He was in fact more concerned over this problem than were the companies themselves.[56] Accordingly, he discussed it soon after his arrival with both President Santos and the Minister of National

53. *T.*, Aug. 30, 1940; Braden to Secretary of State, Sept. 4, 1940, DS 821.6363/1363.

54. *S.*, Jan. 24, 1941.

55. Braden to Secretary of State, May 4, 1939, DS 821.504/109, and June 26, 1939, DS 821.6363/1313. On Colombian Petroleum cf. also *R.*, Jan. 14, 1939. This is not to say that Tropical was spared all criticism, but it was likely to be attacked for less lurid sins, such as charging excessive domestic prices (*S.*, March 1 and 5, 1941).

56. Braden to Secretary of State, Feb. 20, 1940, DS 821.6363/1346.

Economy, and he felt his remarks might have influenced a resolution of the Ministry which reversed, in favor of Socony, a previous ruling that denied the concession sought by a subsidiary on the ground that it would violate hectarage limitations. The new resolution contained an admission that a strict interpretation of the law would be virtually impossible to enforce.[57] A later decree, issued in August, 1939, sought to clarify the hectarage provision further in a sense favorable to the oil companies, and the Minister felt that this solved the problem. Yet Braden remained unconvinced, and his fears seemed confirmed when responsibility for petroleum regulation was shifted to the newly created Ministry of Mines and Petroleum whose first incumbent Minister, Juan Pablo Manotas, categorically expressed the view that existing subsidiary practices were illegal.[58]

Manotas did not propose to do anything about the situation, but his attitude gave weight to Braden's thesis that legislative action was the only solution, both to clear up the hectarage problem for good and to make other needed revisions in the regulatory structure of the petroleum industry. The Minister himself agreed that legal changes were desirable. However, he opposed new legislation, and almost certainly one reason was the administration's fear of reopening the petroleum question in Congress at a time when it was having enough trouble on other fronts with both Conservatives and *lopista* Liberals.[59]

In due course, Braden chose to take the matter up with Foreign Minister López de Mesa, who in turn placed it before a full cabinet meeting late in 1940. The decision was made to seek legislative action, and Manotas took charge of preparing a draft for submission to Congress, paying close attention to the recommendations of oil company representatives.[60] This favorable development was followed by still another when the Ministry of Mines and Petroleum agreed to allow the relinquishment of worthless concessions without insisting on the drilling requirement. But the full cabinet again decided otherwise, this time in a sense unfavorable to the companies.[61] The outcome of the effort to frame new legislation

57. Braden to Secretary of State, March 3, 1939, DS 711.21/931, and April 25, 1939, DS 821.6363/1310.

58. Braden to Secretary of State, Sept. 21, 1939, and Aug. 19, 1940, DS 821.6363/1324, 1360. Cf. *MemMinas* (1940), p. ix.

59. Braden to Secretary of State, Oct. 18, 1940, DS 821.6363/1367.

60. Braden to Secretary of State, Dec. 23, 1940, DS 821.6363/1370.

61. Braden to Secretary of State, March 24, 1941, DS 821.6363/1375.

was another disappointment, since the proposal actually submitted to Congress, in its 1941 sessions, concerned only one relatively minor aspect of petroleum law. The proposal was offered essentially as a trial balloon, to test Congressional reaction, and to Braden it was just one more example of administration "timidity and vacillation."[62] It may also have been, at least in part, a reflection of Colombian annoyance with the oil companies, which among other things had failed to maintain agreement among themselves on exactly what changes were needed.[63] In any event, the proposal failed to gain enactment before Congress adjourned. The administration then proceeded to introduce a different measure the following year, just a few weeks before Santos left office. It was broader in scope, dealing with both the hectarage-limitation and drilling problems, but it also contained some features that the companies found disturbing; and it too failed to pass.[64]

In the end, therefore, the efforts of the United States government and private companies to obtain what they considered a satisfactory solution to the problems facing the oil industry were no more successful than the similar efforts expended on bananas. Braden had even gone so far as to suggest a possible connection between, say, the hectarage-limitation problem and the granting of United States credits to Colombia,[65] but presumably he was not taken very seriously on this point. At least some of the oil companies, meanwhile, had been expressing their dissatisfactions by a gradual slowing down of operations.[66] However, their problems had been less serious to begin with than those of the United Fruit Company. Not only did Tropical continue its production activities without interruption, but Colombian Petroleum's Barco concession finally entered the stage of large-scale production, and with the completion of a pipeline to the Caribbean coast—which entered into service in October, 1939—began to make its contribution to the export market.[67] In 1941, the last full year of the Santos administration, total petroleum exports were valued at 40,525,783 pesos as against 37,206,478 in 1938.[68] The oil industry, which had

---

62. Braden to Secretary of State, Aug. 5, 1941, DS 821.6363/1381.

63. Braden to Secretary of State, Feb. 10, 1941, DS 821.6363/1374.

64. Braden to Secretary of State, March 3, 1942, and Keith to Secretary of State, July 24, 1942, DS 821.6363/1389, 1397.

65. Braden to Secretary of State, Sept. 3, 1940, DS 821.00/1294.

66. See, e.g., Braden to Secretary of State, Aug. 19 and Oct. 18, 1940, DS 821.6363/1360, 1367.

67. *MemMinas* (1940), p. viii.

68. See Appendix.

thus withstood the loss of continental European markets, ultimately felt its share of wartime dislocations, in the form of difficulties in obtaining equipment from abroad and a shortage of tankers for the export trade; but at least oil enjoyed a higher priority than bananas, and these troubles did not fully come to a head until the time of the next administration.[69]

69. Lane to Secretary of State, Sept. 5, 1942, DS 821.6363/1405, and Sept. 18, 1942, DS 821.00/1443.

Wartime Relations

URING THE final months of the Santos administration, Colombian-United States relations on almost every front were affected by the fact that the United States was now openly a belligerent in World War II. The impact of this development on the availability of shipping and supplies for the banana and petroleum industries has already been noted in the preceding chapter, but shortages and dislocations were naturally felt elsewhere too. Political and military relationships similarly entered upon a new phase, which was marked by an even franker Colombian alignment beside the United States than previously existed. Though Colombia did not follow the example of the Central American and Caribbean island republics in automatically declaring war on the Axis powers after the United States had done so, there was little practical difference in the degree of her solidarity.

I

Colombia broke relations with Japan the very day after Pearl Harbor,[1] and on December 18, 1941, President Santos announced in a radio address that his government was also breaking relations

1. *La guerra mundial y la política internacional de Colombia* (Bogotá, 1941), pp. 3-4.

103

with Germany and Italy. On that occasion he explained that he was not proposing a declaration of war because Colombia was "not a military power which could make the weight of its forces appreciably felt in the present struggle and we shall not declare war against anyone who does not attack us directly."[2] It was even unlikely, he added, that such an attack would occur. Yet, according to Santos, Colombia's democratic faith and commitment to inter-American solidarity—not to mention the specific declaration of mutual opposition to extra-continental aggression adopted at the Havana Conference—precluded any kind of passive neutrality in the present critical hour of the United States.[3] The rupture with the Axis was thus only one sign among many of where Colombia's official sympathy lay. Another was the decree issued four days later granting to those American nations which had declared war nonbelligerent status as far as Colombia was concerned.[4] Still another was the strong support for a collective rupture between the American republics and the Axis which was offered by the Colombian delegation to the Rio de Janeiro Conference early in 1942.[5]

Nor was Colombia's response limited to statements of solidarity and diplomatic gestures. Ambassador Braden, who had often lamented what he considered Colombian inefficiency and complacency in dealing with the Axis threat, had to admit that after December 7, 1941, the Colombian authorities were "galvanized into energetic and surprisingly effective action against the totalitarians."[6] This involved, for one thing, a sudden upsurge of official interest in the problem of internal subversion and espionage, even though Santos in his address on Colombia's break with the Axis observed that Colombia "until now had no complaint" about the conduct of resident Axis nationals.[7] Thus a decree issued on December 19 empowered the National Police to dissolve clubs and associations whose activities were presumed contrary to public order, to place strict limitations on the movement of foreign nationals, and to relocate potentially dangerous individuals anywhere within the country under close surveillance.[8] The latter provision was in-

2. *Ibid.*, p. 14.
3. *Ibid.*, pp. 9-15.
4. *MemRels* (1942), p. xii.
5. *Ibid.*, p. 175.
6. Braden to Welles, Jan. 27, 1942, DS 821.00/1394.
7. *La guerra mundial*, p. 15.
8. *Decretos de carácter extraordinario expedidos por el Organo Ejecutivo en desarrollo de las facultades conferidas por las Leyes 128 y 152 de 1941* (Bogotá, 1942), p. 17.

voked even against a certain German priest, who found himself confined to La Vega, Cundinamarca.[9] On December 20, 1941, the authorities closed down the Bogotá office of the Transocean news agency, detaining some seven employees, including the bureau chief.[10] (The next day Transocean dispatches finally disappeared from the pages of *El Siglo*.) Then, too, a decree of January 29, 1942, suspended the naturalization of naturalized Colombians believed involved in "activities inimical to public order and the national security."[11] The Ministry of Education went about closing German schools, and as a special precaution prohibited the placing on school walls of the portrait of any foreign chief except the Pope.[12] Three foreign restaurants were shut down early in 1942 because they were dangerously near military barracks;[13] and several hundred Axis diplomats and private citizens were removed from the country, although for private citizens the removal was in most cases technically voluntary. Those who had been asked to leave were allowed to stay if they protested strongly enough.[14]

Additional measures, adopted in January, 1942, established controls over the assets belonging to citizens of either Axis or Axis-occupied countries, which were in certain cases to be placed under a government-supervised trust administration.[15] One purpose of the latter procedure was to Colombianize Axis-owned business firms at least for the duration of the war, so that they could be removed from the British and United States Proclaimed Lists and thus again function normally. The control exercised over assets belonging to individual Axis nationals who were resident in Colombia was at first rather slight, but it was made more extensive later in the year, following the incident of June 23, 1942, in which a German submarine sank the Colombian schooner *Resolute* traveling between the Caribbean coast and the Colombian island group of San Andrés and Providencia. The fact that survivors adrift in a lifeboat were machine-gunned from the submarine added to Colombian indignation over the incident. It was officially explained

9. *L.*, Jan. 22, 1942.

10. *L.*, Dec. 21, 1941.

11. Edward N. Barnhart, "Citizenship and Political Tests in Latin American Republics in World War II," *Hispanic American Historical Review*, XVII (August, 1962), 326.

12. *L.*, Jan. 22 and 30, 1942; *Revista Javeriana*, XVII (March, 1942), "Suplemento," 62.

13. *L.*, Jan. 22, 1942.

14. *MemRels* (1942), pp. 222-23, 248-49, 290.

15. *Decretos de carácter extraordinario*, pp. 42-48, 64-69.

that the new financial controls that were decreed just two days later, freezing all assets of Axis nationals in Colombia, were not taken in reprisal but were only precautionary. However, this did not make them less onerous; and they coincided with another order requiring Axis nationals to evacuate not only Colombian coastal areas but even Magdalena River ports.[16]

The Colombian government was also prepared to honor a growing number of requests for cooperation from the armed forces of the United States. When the United States War Department indicated a desire to station light observation planes at Villavicencio on the Colombian *llanos*, for surveillance against possible "secret airfields" or other suspicious activities, President Santos readily gave his approval, stipulating only that no military uniforms or insignia should be in evidence. In the end the United States failed to take advantage of this permission, even though a scheme had been mutually agreed upon to satisfy Santos's condition by attaching both planes and personnel in an ostensibly civilian capacity to American petroleum companies that were doing exploratory work of their own on the *llanos*.[17] A request to station United States military and naval observers at Barranquilla, Medellín, and Cúcuta was handled, again with Santos's express approval, in roughly comparable fashion, except that this time the plan was implemented. The observers were simply attached as "assistants" to the United States consulates at the cities in question, though at Cúcuta, where there was no consulate, one had to be created for the occasion.[18] In May, 1942, the Colombian War Ministry even went so far as to give permission—orally—for the establishment of a fueling base for United States military aircraft on Providencia Island. In this case gasoline barrels were to be consigned to Pan American Airways, which would be the theoretical beneficiary of

16. *MemRels* (1942), pp. xvii-xix; *MemHda* (1942), pp. 47-60; *Decretos de carácter extraordinario*, pp. 376-78; *L.*, June 26, 1942. The freeze was not, of course, absolute—e.g., bank accounts could be drawn upon for a small daily amount to cover necessary living expenses.

17. Braden to Secretary of State, Dec. 24, 1941, DS 810.20 Defense/1826; Secretary of State to Braden, Feb. 18, 1942, and Braden to Secretary of State, Feb. 20, 1942, *FR* (1942), VI, 142, 145-46; Keith to Secretary of State, March 16, 1942, DS 821.20/197; Lane to Secretary of State, May 6, 1942, DS 810.20 Defense/2656. Actually the United States at this time obtained "virtually unrestricted flying and photographic privileges for United States military planes," though "without the formality of new written agreements" (Conn and Fairchild, *Framework of Hemisphere Defense*, p. 263).

18. Secretary of State to Braden, Feb. 19, 1942, and Braden to Secretary of State, same date, *FR* (1942), VI, 142-44.

the arrangement; but in practice military planes were given the right to fly over and land on the island without restriction.[19] Such subterfuges as these (and there were others) were actually rather transparent; even the true function of the consular assistants was soon an open secret.[20] They did, however, maintain a façade of Colombian nonbelligerency, and they appear to have been valued for this purpose by the Santos administration.

The Providencia "base" was designed primarily, of course, as a support facility for anti-submarine operations in the Caribbean. These operations were of special interest to Colombia because of the threat posed by submarine warfare to her own foreign trade, over and above considerations of democratic sympathy with the United States. Thus Colombia also adopted measures to protect the secrecy of shipping movements to and from her ports,[21] and was happy to send officials to the United States to receive special training in radio-station detection, precisely so that they could help weed out clandestine transmitters that might be giving information to German raiders.[22]

The United States, on its part, was interested in establishing guidelines to deal with a somewhat broader range of possible military operations in the Caribbean area. Under the staff agreements worked out earlier with Colombia, United States forces were already committed to assist Colombia, on request, in repelling any sort of extra-continental threat to her sovereignty; but if such a threat should materialize in the vicinity of Colombian coastal areas and territorial waters there was no assurance that a formal request for help could be presented in time. Hence in February, 1942, the United States proposed that Colombia station a liaison officer at the Canal Zone so as to be ready for any such emergency. Colombia promptly agreed to sending the liaison officer, who was accredited as military attaché to Panama. If the situation presented itself, he was authorized to give "definite" approval to an emergency military action involving entry of United States forces into Colombian territory or waters, but Santos insisted that it would still be necessary for him to obtain formal confirmation by radio from Bogotá, since the President could not constitutionally delegate his own power of final decision. Such a solution was not

19. Lane to Secretary of State, May 11, 1942, *FR* (1942), VI, 150.
20. See, e.g., Lane memo, July 25, 1942, *FR* (1942), VI, 155.
21. *Decretos de carácter extraordinario*, pp. 35-36.
22. Memo, Bonsal to Welles, July 15, 1942, DS 711.21/959.

entirely satisfactory to the military authorities in the Canal Zone, but Colombia refused to yield the point of principle involved. Instead, the government at Bogotá ultimately fell back on a very typical stratagem: it merely instructed its liaison officer not to make an issue, in practice, over any emergency operation of this sort by United States forces. Once the emergency action was taken against the enemy, further measures could then be discussed through regular channels.[23]

Obviously, there was still an element of ambiguity in the right of trespass thus tacitly accorded to United States forces. The one point most emphatically clarified by Santos himself was that United States naval and air units could enter or fly over Colombian waters at any time in direct pursuit of enemy craft. He made exception only in the case of an enemy submarine immobilized by Colombian forces in a Colombian port—and as usual he gave his authorization orally rather than in writing.[24]

During the first half of 1942 Colombia also entered into two formal military agreements with the United States that were both committed to writing and publicly acknowledged. One, signed on May 29, 1942, was an enlargement of the 1938 aviation agreement which converted it into a full-scale army mission agreement for the purpose of providing technical assistance to Colombian land forces as well as military aviation. This was, at least in part, the mere ratification of a situation that already existed.[25] The other agreement was the long-delayed lend-lease pact, which was finally signed on March 17, 1942.[26] Its terms were essentially similar to those of the draft agreement first presented to Colombia in July, 1941, whose consideration had bogged down amid both substantive and legalistic objections. However, negotiations were reactivated in the new mood of urgency that resulted from Pearl

23. Acting Secretary of State (Welles) to Braden, Feb. 20, 1942, Braden to Secretary of State, Feb. 21, 1942, and Lane to Secretary of State, April 30 and May 5, 1942, *FR* (1942), VI, 144-49.

24. Lane to Secretary of State, May 22, 1942, *FR* (1942), VI, 152.

25. *Military Mission. Agreement Between the United States of America and Colombia* (Executive Agreement Series No. 250; Washington, 1942); above, p. 13. The original aviation mission agreement had already been renewed, on an interim basis, pending completion of the new one (*Military Mission Agreement Between the United States of America and Colombia Continuing in Effect the Agreement of November 23, 1938* [Executive Agreement Series No. 237; Washington, 1942]).

26. *FR* (1942), VI, 189-92; above, pp. 55-57.

Harbor,[27] and the emergency powers which were voted to the Colombian Executive on December 13, 1941—and which provided the principal legal basis for the extraordinary measures so far discussed[28]—apparently removed Santos's doubts as to his government's authority to approve the agreement. Specifically, it provided for the United States to supply "defense articles" to Colombia "to a value of about $16,200,000," which would be repaid without interest and at a discount of 55.56 per cent. It made no provision, direct or indirect, for the "free" funds that Colombia had been seeking in addition to the lend-lease equipment itself, but the United States did agree, informally and on at least a temporary basis, to absorb the freight costs which would normally have been paid by the recipient country.[29] On the other hand, Colombia never made any attempt to use the entire $16.2 million authorization. During all the rest of World War II she was to take only $6.5 million, approximately, in lend-lease equipment;[30] and most of this was received after Santos left office.

The transfer of equipment was not wholly one way: on August 6, 1942, the last full day of the Santos administration, Colombia transferred to the United States two tankers that represented a modest contribution toward easing the critical shipping shortage of the period.[31] These were originally Italian tankers that took refuge in the harbor of Cartagena during June, 1941. Colombia had been trying to buy them outright from their owners, but the price asked was impossibly high, and while purchase negotiations dragged on, the vessels deteriorated. Argentina was also interested in ultimately acquiring the tankers from Colombia, but after Pearl Harbor the United States made an urgent plea to take them over immediately and get them back into service. Santos was as usual willing to oblige, ordering all consideration of other proposals terminated forthwith.[32]

---

27. Braden to Secretary of State, Dec. 15, 1941, *FR* (1941), VII, 35-38. At this point Foreign Minister López de Mesa submitted the all-time high in military aid requests, amounting to $16.2 million in equipment plus another $6,450,000 in funds for roads, uniforms, and the like; but he was quickly discouraged by Braden.

28. *Decretos de carácter extraordinario*, pp. 5-9 and *passim*.

29. Memo, Bonsal to Welles, July 15, 1942, DS 711.21/959.

30. *N.Y.T.*, June 14, 1946, 11:5.

31. *FR* (1942), VI, 204n.

32. *MemRels* (1942), pp. xxxv-xxxvi; Braden to Secretary of State, Dec. 25, 1941, DS 800.85/512, and Jan. 2 and 9, 1942, *FR* (1942), VI, 193-94.

Nevertheless, the transfer took some time to arrange. For one thing, Colombia sought a reciprocal pledge from the United States to deliver one or two ordinary merchant ships for use by Colombia or to guarantee a certain minimum allocation of tonnage to Colombian trade. In this matter the United States was willing only to promise that it would do what it could to meet Colombia's shipping needs, and Colombia reluctantly yielded the point. The other principal difficulty concerned Colombia's inability to take prior possession of the tankers on any terms Italy would accept and her consequent fear of being faced with excessive claims for reimbursement after the war was over if she now seized them unilaterally. There was a simple solution to this problem: the United States could guarantee to accept full responsibility for whatever amount Colombia might ultimately be obliged, by arbitration or otherwise, to pay the original owners. The United States Embassy in Bogotá considered such a guarantee perfectly reasonable, and Colombian financial qualms made it almost inevitable, but officials in Washington (where several different agencies were involved) were surprisingly slow in coming around to terms Colombia felt she could accept. Not until June, 1942, did both sides formally agree that the War Shipping Administration should purchase the tankers for $1,500,000 plus any additional amount Colombia might later have to pay the Italians. A few more weeks were then spent on further detailed arrangements, and the transfer was consummated, as mentioned, on August 6.[33]

Another material contribution by Colombia to the United States war effort—easier to arrange—was a joint agreement to promote the gathering of wild rubber and to sell the entire Colombian output, less what was needed for domestic manufacturing, to the United States. A proposal to this effect was submitted to the Colombian government by the Rubber Reserve Company (which was an official agency) in March, 1942, along the lines of a similar agreement made with Brazil. Colombia immediately expressed interest, and even before the completion of negotiations had placed an embargo on rubber exports except to the United States government.[34]

33. Select documents on the U.S.-Colombian tanker negotiations are found in *FR* (1942), VI, 193-204. The actual purchase contract was not signed, however, until July 30, 1943; see *FR* (1943), VI, 37-43.

34. Secretary of State to Keith, March 23, 1942, Keith to Secretary of State, March 25, 1942, and Lane to Secretary of State, June 6, 1942, *FR* (1942), VI, 170-72, 183.

One point that had to be ironed out was naturally the price, but an obvious guideline was the price the United States would be paying to Brazil, a much larger supplier. Thus in the end the Colombian price was made the same as the Brazilian except for one type of rubber (Castilloa) for which Colombia was offered somewhat better terms. A minor complication appeared when an Argentine buyer sought to purchase a quantity of Castilloa rubber at a still higher price, but after this offer had been briefly used for bargaining purposes it was turned aside in favor of the United States, whose proposal had offsetting advantages. The latter was for an extended period (ultimately set at five years), and it included the pledge of a special development fund to help provide rubber-gathering launches, road construction, and related facilities for the encouragement of rubber production.

The other major aspect of the rubber negotiations—and here there was a close parallel with the earlier and somewhat comparable platinum-purchase transaction, in which loss of Japanese silk supplies was a troublesome side effect—was the attempt of Colombia to extract some *quid pro quo* in the form of protection against wartime shortages. Colombia thus asked to know whether, as part of the arrangement, the United States would provide equipment for establishing a domestic tire manufacturing plant to meet at least part of the nation's tire needs; and in fact in Colombia as in several other Latin American republics private United States companies had already submitted proposals to construct such a plant. Colombia also asked for guarantees that her immediate requirements would be met by deliveries from abroad. Officials in Washington, however, felt that a proliferation of new tire plants was not an efficient approach to the problem—quite apart from the difficulty of obtaining the needed equipment—and that in the specific case of Colombia, plant construction would represent unnecessary duplication of manufacturing capacity already existing in Venezuela. Thus the United States government would offer to cooperate toward the establishment of a tire plant only in so far as "exigencies of the present international emergency" permitted, and for the rest it would guarantee delivery of a given quantity of tires to Colombia *provided* shipping and the desired sizes and types were available. As in the other negotiations, Colombia realistically settled for such promises to do whatever was possible. A formal contract was thus signed on July 1, 1942, on behalf of the Rubber Reserve Company and the Caja de Crédito Agrario, which was to be in charge of the rubber-development program at the Colombian end and the sole intermediary for buying up Colombian production.[35]

The inability to give firm assurances of the delivery of essential imports was disappointing even if understandable, and the shortages that in fact appeared in Colombia were a source of continuing irritation, part of which was inevitably directed against the United States.[36] For this reason, and also to make sure that Colombian demands were kept at a reasonable level by efficient distribution and use of what actually was made available, the United States Embassy had repeatedly urged the Colombian government to tighten its own administrative procedures. And in this respect, too, the Santos regime was "galvanized into action" in the aftermath of December 7. A series of executive decrees established special regulations for the control of scarce commodities like tires and iron and steel, and in February, 1942, the Superintendencia Nacional de Importaciones was created to provide more efficient centralized direction in this area. The latter was frankly designed to satisfy the urgings of the United States. Among other things, it was to supply the data needed by United States agencies in determining priorities and export quotas for Colombia, issue certificates of necessity for Colombian importers, and govern the distribution of essential imports within the country. Many of its functions had been previously entrusted to the Oficina de Comercio e Industrias of the Ministry of National Economy, but they had not received that bureau's sole attention. The same decree that created the Superintendencia also established a Departamento Comercial in the Colombian Embassy in Washington, precisely to help expedite the issuance of export licenses. All these (and similar) measures did not eliminate the economic dislocations created by the war, but they made them at least a little more tolerable,

---

35. Documents on the rubber negotiations will be found in *FR* (1942), VI, 170-89; see also *MemEcNac* (1942), pp. 167-69. The United States was also supplying seed and technical assistance to Colombia for the production of plantation, as distinct from wild, rubber (*MemEcNac* [1942], p. 103); but the time required for plantings to come into production was too great for this particular program to have any substantial practical results before the end of the war.

36. For a call for greater understanding of the difficulties faced by the United States, see the editorial in *L.*, Nov. 21, 1941, which recognized Colombian impatience with supply shortages and other such problems as a major source of friction between the two countries.

and they facilitated working relationships with the United States in economic and commercial matters.[37]

II

The Colombian official response to the United States' direct involvement in World War II met a wide degree of political approval within the country. All Liberal factions supported the President in breaking relations with the Axis and in the other measures short of a declaration of war whereby he aligned Colombia almost unrestrictedly with the United States. Alfonso López had private reservations concerning some of Santos's equally private informal arrangements of military cooperation, including the opening given to United States forces to enter Colombian territory in certain circumstances, but he did not oppose the objectives. He merely questioned the methods, which he considered to be of doubtful constitutionality and a possible source of adverse political repercussions later on. He thus hoped that when he took office as president for a second term he would be able to place Santos's commitments on a firm, frank, and legal basis. He pledged to continue them in effect until that was done.[38]

Strong expressions of support for the embattled United States and for the administration's policy toward the conflict were also forthcoming from the more moderate and pro-American elements of the Conservative Party. *El Colombiano* of Medellín duly traced Colombia's basic sympathy for the United States back to Marco Fidel Suárez, thus giving a proper Conservative aura to the latest measures of Eduardo Santos.[39] In Bogotá, Roberto Urdaneta Arbeláez gathered the signatures of several dozen prominent Conservatives during the latter part of December, 1941, for a public statement of support for administration foreign policy.[40] Some of the signers were men who a year before had suffered in silence while Laureano Gómez was launching vitriolic assaults upon the

37. *MemHda* (1942), pp. 28-40; *MemEcNac* (1942), pp. 83-85; *Decretos de carácter extraordinario*, pp. 138-41 and *passim*. The Superintendencia Nacional de Importaciones was at first located administratively within the Ministry of National Economy but later was moved to the Ministry of Finance.

38. Lane to Secretary of State, May 26, 1942, and Lane memo, July 25, 1942, *FR* (1942), VI, 153-56; Lane to Secretary of State, Aug. 19, 1942, DS 821.20/213.

39. Cited in *L.*, Dec. 18, 1941.

40. *L.*, Dec. 21, 1941; *S.*, Dec. 29, 1941.

Good Neighbor; now at last they were prepared to stand up and be counted.

Gómez himself was not among the signers. Neither was he among the substantial group of Conservative Congressmen who voted in favor of the extraordinary faculties granted to the administration in December, 1941, so that it could adopt measures for the new emergency by executive decree.[41] Indeed his newspaper proceeded to take part in the airing of old charges that depicted Urdaneta as an errand boy of North American business interests, and it denounced the infliction on peaceful German nationals of "every sort of abuses allegedly in defense of [our] endangered sovereignty."[42] Yet *El Siglo* still found time to express admiration for Ambassador Braden,[43] and it offered few if any comments that could be considered overtly anti-American. Fundamentally it simply continued to follow a neutralist line after as before Pearl Harbor, and to criticize the Santos administration for making major decisions on international policy all by itself and then expecting Congress and the nation to accept them as *faits accomplis*. It was on this basis that *El Siglo* in due course attacked the break in relations with the Axis powers,[44] although initially it had expressed no editorial opinion on the move.

In any event, Laureano Gómez was less concerned with World War II than with the Colombian presidential election that was scheduled for the first Sunday in May, 1942. He did not consider the time yet ripe to offer a Conservative candidate, but he did propose to see what advantage could be taken of the continuing split in Liberal ranks. Santos himself and most of the top echelon of *santista* Liberals had reconciled themselves to the unavoidable prospect of López's re-election, but there was also an irreconcilable wing of Liberals who for reasons of political philosophy or presumed factional advantage or sheer personal antipathy toward López insisted on presenting a dissident Liberal candidate. The latter role was gladly accepted by Dr. Carlos Arango Vélez, and Gómez saw to it that he received vigorous Conservative backing. As far as domestic issues were concerned, such endorsement was logical enough: Arango Vélez was definitely on the right wing of his party. What gave Gómez's position a special touch of irony was

41. *L.*, Dec. 18 and 20, 1941.
42. *S.*, Dec. 28, 1941.
43. *S.*, Dec. 19, 1941.
44. *S.*, Jan. 23, 24, and 27, 1942.

the fact that Arango Vélez had been a consistent and seemingly unconditional supporter of close ties with the United States. If he had any quarrel with the inter-American policy of Santos, it was that Santos had not gone far enough. This, however, did not perturb Laureano Gómez. He never claimed to agree with all the views of the candidate he supported; he believed in the primacy of domestic problems; and in the field of foreign policy he ostensibly preferred a lackey of the United States who was honest and consistent to a sheer opportunist, as he felt López to be.[45]

Foreign policy thus did not play a clear-cut role in the 1942 election campaign. Arango Vélez had been attacking López ever since the latter's Hotel Granada speech of January, 1941, on the ground that López was not a trustworthy proponent of hemispheric solidarity;[46] yet he himself was supported for the presidency by a Conservative Party many of whose leading spokesmen either did not believe in hemispheric solidarity at all or gave it a very narrow definition of their own. Only near the end of the campaign did the relationship between Colombia and the United States briefly become the leading topic of debate, and this development was actually somewhat fortuitous. It began when Arango Vélez gave an interview to the Associated Press in which he was quoted as saying, among other things: "I am unmistakably in favor of an 'all out' assistance to the countries now waging war against totalitarian aggression; and I consider that the best way in which Colombia can make her cooperation felt . . . is by putting the country on a military footing, and by doing so immediately. It is obvious that we cannot go out and fight Germany or Japan ourselves, but it is no less true to say that this country has been allowed to live and think as if it was at peace, when the truth is that aggression is nearer—much nearer—to us, than what the Colombians believe. The defense of the Panama Canal should not be regarded as something that we are supposed to undertake, as a friendly help to the United States, but as something as vital to us, as it is to them. . . . I know that the only way in which we can give material help is by providing the human element for this defense; and by accepting the technical military guidance of the United States. I go even further in this, by saying that the

45. This general line of reasoning is well set forth in the lead editorial of S., April 28, 1941, which undoubtedly reflects Gómez's own views on the matter.
46. See, e.g., T., Feb. 11, 1941.

best possible intelligence service obtainable abroad should be made available to guard our country against any and all possible fifth columns and espionage dangers that may [be]—and are—lurking in our midst."[47]

This interview was intended for publication abroad, and not before the day of the elections, May 3; but the *lopista* organ *El Liberal* obtained a copy of it and broke the story on April 27.[48] Despite the efforts of Arango Vélez to hedge or clarify certain points after the interview was printed—emphasizing, for instance, that he did *not* mean for Colombian troops to be sent to the Canal Zone—the net effect of the affair was obviously harmful to his candidacy.[49] The impetuous tone of the candidate's remarks was enough to raise the eyebrows even of many sincere friends of the United States, while diehard anti-Yankees in the Conservative camp were given another good reason, if they were looking for one, to refuse to vote as Gómez instructed. But the stand of Gómez himself was not affected. *El Siglo,* in its comments, recognized the existence of foreign-policy differences between Arango Vélez and his Conservative backers—just as the candidate had recognized them in the course of the famous interview—but it gave credit to Arango for forthrightness while pointing to *El Liberal's* journalistic coup as a typical example of *lopista* trickery.[50]

Be that as it may, Gómez's support of Arango Vélez was still another reason for playing down, at least for the present, whatever anti-American sentiments lingered in his breast. At the same time, López, in his capacity as official candidate of the ruling party, found himself generally assuming the defense of Santos's foreign policy. He and his supporters did not exploit the Arango Vélez interview for purposes of crude anti-American propaganda, as *El Siglo* would surely have done at one point, but were content to see it used against the person interviewed, who in the end carried only the Departments of Caldas, Cauca, Valle del Cauca, and Huila. Even so, he gathered 41 per cent of the vote on a nationwide basis. It was not a bad showing, especially in view of the advantages, licit and illicit, that were enjoyed by the Liberal Party machine. An analysis of the voting patterns at least demonstrates that Gómez's willingness to overlook his candidate's blatant pro-

47. *L.,* April 30, 1942, giving the English text.
48. *L.,* April 27 and 28, 1942.
49. *R.,* April 28, 1942; Lane to Secretary of State, May 2, 1942, DS 821.00/1411.
50. *S.,* April 28, 1942, and *passim.*

Americanism was shared by a majority of the Conservative rank-and-file.[51]

To be sure, a latent strain of anti-Americanism still persisted in Conservative ranks, as could readily be seen in some of the reactions to the sinking of the *Resolute* in June, 1942. Throughout Colombia city councils and departmental assemblies adopted a flood of protest resolutions, and *El Siglo*, though it had no part in the more extreme anti-Nazi tub-thumping, referred to the sinking as a "barbarous aggression."[52] Yet there were other Conservatives who in one way or another openly sought to use the incident as a springboard for attacking the Santos administration and indirectly the United States. Their line of reasoning was that the sinking was a regrettable but logical corollary of the unneutral stand taken by Colombia in tying herself irrevocably to United States interests. A Conservative speaker in the Cundinamarca assembly even cited the "American" names of the victims—which reflected the status of San Andrés and Providencia as an English-speaking enclave under the Colombian flag—as further reason for minimizing the incident,[53] while the Conservative newspaper *El Norte* of Cúcuta publicized a rumor suggesting that the aggressor had actually been a United States rather than a German submarine.[54] At the same time, however, Conservatives of the Urdaneta Arbeláez variety, together with Liberal spokesmen, naturally took the occasion to express once again their solidarity with the Santos administration in the conduct of foreign affairs and with the United States in its struggle against totalitarianism.

III

Spruille Braden, who took up duties in Bogotá a few months after Santos's inauguration, departed in March, 1942, for a new assignment in Havana, just a few months before Santos left office. He received the tribute of a large farewell banquet at which Alfonso López paid homage to inter-American solidarity, and even one of the "Gómez clique" (as Braden put it) was present.[55] Moreover, to his successor Arthur Bliss Lane, who pre-

---

51. *Memoria del Ministro de Gobierno . . . 1942*, I, 71-99, gives the complete returns by departments and municipalities.

52. S., June 26, 1942; L., June 27-29, 1942.

53. *La Defensa* (Medellín), June 25, 1942; S. and L., June 27, 1942.

54. Keith to Secretary of State, July 10, 1942, DS 800.20210/1262.

55. *N.Y.T.*, March 10, 1942, 4:7; Braden to Welles, Jan. 27, 1942, DS 821.00/1394.

sented his credentials to Eduardo Santos on April 30,[56] he left Colombian-United States relations in remarkably favorable condition. As Braden observed in one of the last memoranda he wrote as Ambassador to Colombia, with specific reference to military cooperation, but speaking also of the entire relationship between the two countries, Colombia "has not asked for all of the $16,000,000 Lend-Lease credit. In other words, she has not endeavored to obtain excessive or unfair exactions from us . . . but has made a sound and conservative estimate of what are her military requirements. Otherwise, as I have before stated, we have obtained *everything* that we have sought in this country. Colombia was the first South American nation to break relations with Germany and has endeavored to influence the neighboring state of Venezuela to follow suit. In short, if a balance sheet were to be made of what has been done respectively by the United States and Colombia, it would show that Colombia has not bargained but has wholeheartedly come through in support of our policies in a manner which, if anything, places us under an indebtedness to Colombia and there is *no* country in South America which has performed more cooperatively."[57]

Braden exaggerated at some points in the preceding passage, which was written to refute what he considered some unwarranted quibbling by his acting military attaché. Colombia's estimates of her military requirements had not all been "sound and conservative," even though sound conservatism may have triumphed in the end. Colombia had done a certain amount of bargaining, even if not very hard bargaining, and one reason the United States obtained "everything" that was asked was that the Embassy in Bogotá had a good idea of how far the Santos administration was prepared to go in Good Neighborly collaboration and did not formally request what Santos was likely to refuse. Nevertheless, the Ambassador's statement contained substantially more truth than exaggeration.

Actually, from the standpoint of the United States, the specific acts of cooperation sought and obtained from Colombia were seldom of major importance in themselves. It was good to have Colombian assistance in providing material necessities for the war effort, but Colombia was not a key supplier of any strategic article

56. *FR* (1942), VI, 147*n*.
57. Braden, memo, March 6, 1942, attached to dispatch of Keith to Secretary of State, March 16, 1942, DS 821.20/197. Italics are Braden's.

except platinum. It was certainly desirable to have Colombia's express permission to enter her waters in pursuit of enemy submarines, but even without such permission it is hard to conceive that the United States Navy would have allowed Colombian waters to become a privileged sanctuary. And though United States holders of defaulted Colombian bonds were mostly glad to see the resumption of service, the sums involved were not really large, nor was there any escaping the fact that the initial payments were financed, indirectly, by the Export-Import Bank. What was of primary interest to the United States, in the last analysis, was to have the South American nation closest to the Panama Canal in the hands of a stable and friendly administration, so that additional energies and resources that were urgently needed elsewhere would not have to be devoted to guarding the Canal's southern flank. There were occasional doubts—mostly exaggerated—as to the stability of the Santos regime, but never the slightest doubt as to its friendship. In this respect, therefore, Colombia fully earned the praise lavished by Ambassador Braden.

The benefits accruing to Colombia in return for her cooperation were also both tangible and intangible. Under the former heading there were Export-Import Bank loans, military assistance, and the assistance of the United States in drawing up and implementing the 1940 coffee agreement. There were beginnings of other technical and economic aid, as in the rubber agreement, and undoubtedly a greater effort was made to keep Colombia supplied with essential imports than would have been the case with an unfriendly administration in Bogotá, although precisely how much difference friendship made would be hard to measure. On the borderline between tangible and intangible benefits there was the friendly intercession of the United States government on Colombia's behalf not only with foreign bondholders but with American businesses operating in Colombia, although in the case of the banana industry that intercession was obviously not enough. There was, finally, the benefit to Colombia of the United States' political and military efforts against the Axis dictatorships. This would be a tangible benefit if it meant warding off a real threat of attack on Colombia, which few Colombians believed to exist. However, Eduardo Santos sided with the United States on the international scene primarily because he believed from the very first moment that the world would be a better place for Colombians (and everyone) to live in if the democratic powers ultimately prevailed over their antagonists. This was largely an intangible benefit, but in Santos's opinion it was even worth a few sacrifices.

The picture of Colombian-United States cooperation during the 1938-1942 period was naturally just one aspect of the generally healthy condition of inter-American relations. The Good Neighbor Policy was in its heyday and was being intensified and expanded in many directions in order to assure the United States government of Latin American friendship as it prepared to do battle on other fronts. The cordial response evoked in Colombia, however, was particularly gratifying, since the Colombian political system, with all its imperfections, came closer to exemplifying the democratic ideals for which the United States claimed to be striving than did the systems of most Latin American nations. The freedom of expression and the constitutional proprieties that existed in Colombia did create some drawbacks. Anti-American sentiments could be voiced more easily than in the average Caribbean dictatorship, and Bryce Wood's observation that the working of the Good Neighbor Policy was more effective in areas subject to the Executive Branch alone[58] was every bit as applicable to Colombia as to the United States. Nevertheless, Colombia and the United States during the Santos administration constructed a framework of relationships that in most respects was eminently successful. At the policy level, they achieved a high degree of mutual understanding, as contrasted with the naïve trustfulness of Olaya Herrera and the comparative reserve of the first López administration. At the level of detailed programs, they introduced new approaches to economic and military cooperation that were geared in considerable part to the crises of the moment but have in effect, for better or worse, become permanent.[59]

58. See, e.g., Bryce Wood, "The Department of State and the Non-National Interest: The Cases of Argentine Meat and Paraguayan Tea," *Inter-American Economic Affairs*, XV (Autumn, 1961), 5.

59. Although the topic of cultural relations was expressly excluded from the present study, it must be noted, for the record, that in this field too there were new departures and a new official emphasis given. Symptomatic was the creation, in 1941, of the post of Senior Cultural Relations Assistant in the United States Embassy in Bogotá, which was first filled by Dr. Herschel Brickell (*N.Y.T.*, Nov. 1, 1941, 4:2).

Appendix

1. Colombian Foreign Trade by Year, in Thousands of Pesos (U.S. percentages in parentheses):

Year	Imports		Exports	
1938	159,252	(51)	163,226	(58)
1939	183,442	(56)	177,053	(67)
1940	148,193	(74)	167,876	(75)
1941	170,006	(77)	176,133	(77)
1942	104,980	(60)	191,902	(92)

2. Major Colombian Exports by Year, Value in Pesos (U.S. percentage in parentheses):

   a) Coffee

1938	88,775,329	(80)
1939	87,124,693	(83)
1940	74,023,042	(93)
1941	83,293,779	(96)
1942	144,750,690	(99)

   b) Gold[1]

1938	18,780,402	(100)
1939	40,582,122	(100)
1940	41,838,427	(100)
1941	42,589,427	(100)
1942	20,965,629	(100)

   c) Petroleum[2]

1938	37,206,478	(0)
1939	31,902,996	(6)
1940	39,919,927	(2)
1941	40,525,783	(15)
1942	14,197,345	(31)

   d) Bananas

1938	8,883,871	(49)
1939	8,678,583	(27)
1940	5,609,752	(48)
1941	2,923,702	(95)
1942	284,006	(99)

Source: *Anuario de comercio exterior.*

1. Gold was not included in Colombian official export totals, but it has been included in those offered above.

2. Petroleum export data do not give a clear picture of ultimate destination, since the leading purchaser was listed as Curaçao except in 1940 and 1941, when it was replaced by Canada. Both France and Italy, however, also appeared as major destinations in the immediate prewar period.

121

Index